MARRIED... *in* BUSINESS

What you must know and achieve to survive and thrive in this all-important partnership

By Jack and Elaine Wyman

Illustrated by Linus Maurer

Published by Doer Publications

Married…in Business
by Jack and Elaine Wyman

First Edition published in 1999
Copyright © 1999 by Jack and Elaine Wyman

All rights reserved. No part of this book may be used or reproduced without written permission from the publisher or copyright holder, except in the case of brief quotations embodied in reviews.

Doer Publications
7950 E. Camelback Rd., #110
Scottsdale, AZ 85251

Cover design by Lisa Johnson, Laguna Beach, California
Cover and interior cartoons by Linus Maurer, Kenwood, California
Interior design by The Printed Page, Phoenix, Arizona
Back cover photograph by Al Jacobs, Scottsdale, Arizona

Publishing Cataloging-in-Publication
(Provided by Quality Books, Inc.)

Wyman, Jack.
Married-- in business : what you must know and achieve to survive and thrive in this all important partnership / by Jack and Elaine Wyman ; illustrated by Linus Maurer. -- 1st ed.
p. cm.
Includes index.
LCCN: 99-094625
ISBN: 0-9639180-0-1

1. Couple-owned business enterprises--United States--Management. 2. Work and family--United States. 3. Interpersonal relations. I. Wyman, Elaine. II. Title.

HD62.27.W96 1999 658′.042
QBI99-150

Manufactured in the United States of America

Dedication

As authors of this book, we dedicate it to (as they say)—the one person without whom it could not have been written—EACH OTHER!

And so we say to each other:

"In our in-depth collaboration you've been funny, frustrating, hard-working, exasperating, inspiring, even brilliant! You've made this intensive project a fulfilling, joyous experience. You're the greatest!"

Disclaimer

The purpose of this book, *Married...In Business*, is to provide helpful background and general information concerning its subject matter. The book is sold with the understanding that the publisher and authors do not render accounting, legal, investment counsel, engineering, marital advice or counseling or hi-tech services. If these services are needed, the help of an able, established professional in the specific field should be sought.

It was not the authors' or publisher's intent that this book contain or reproduce the voluminous information and material that may be available on the subject of being married in business. Nor was it the intent to present anything resembling a text book on the subject. Rather, it is the hope that this lighter, briefer read, with its cartoons and anecdotal approach will begin to inform and entertain sufficiently to awaken interest in the subject, so that readers may enter into a serious exploration of the subject.

As this book states and reiterates, much research, thought, study and conversation should precede the move toward starting up a business with one's spouse. And then, it should be the right business at the right time and in the right place.

Forty-three of the couples whose stories are told in this book were interviewed, and their individual profiles, approved. Their inclusion in these pages are not to be considered endorsements for their products or services. Their stories are presented to give flavor, background and written snapshots of their various businesses and modus operandi.

As in any book of this type, typographical errors and mistakes in content may occur. For these we apologize. May we suggest that you use this book as an idea-starter.

The authors and publishers shall have neither liability nor responsibility to any person or entity with respect to any loss or damage caused, or alleged to be caused, directly or indirectly, by information contained in this book.

Contents

Acknowledgments

To all of the wonderful people who helped us with this book we can only offer an enormous THANK YOU!

Of course, that especially goes for the couples whose stories are presented in the pages that follow. We're glad we know them; we're glad that you're going to meet them.

If we were holding a huge meeting in a vast auditorium, attended by everybody, everywhere who is interested in the subject of being married...in business, we'd announce that there are some wonderful people present that the entire audience must meet. So, let's imagine that we're now going to call their names, and ask them to stand up, be recognized and receive show-stopping applause! Here we go:

First, four fine professional publishing specialists who played very important roles in this book. They are **Ben Lizardi of Pasadena, California** for his overall creative contribution, **Karla Olson** and **Lisa Liddy of Phoenix, Arizona,** and **Lisa Johnson of Laguna Beach, California**. Karla was our able, ever-patient editor, too often interrupted by our questions. Lisa Liddy was our designer, who also must have said to herself, "Oh, it's the Wymans again with more changes." Lisa Johnson designed our all-important cover. We are very grateful to Ben, Karla and the two Lisas. They did fine work and helped immensely.

Paul and Sarah Edwards of Santa Monica, California. The Edwards, recognized leaders in the home-based business movement, gave us valuable answers to our early questions, plus significant encouragement. We sincerely thank them. We are very fortunate to present the Edwards's own story about their relationship in business in the book.

Joyce Bloom of Powell, Wyoming. Joyce, a proven true friend from 'way, 'way back, not only kept up our spirits with her ever-ready sense of humor, but she personally contacted a group of very special people in Wyoming, Utah and Wisconsin, most of whom ended up with stories in our book. We'll never be able to thank Joyce enough!

Dave Morse of Rockland, Maine. Dave, with whom Jack did marketing consulting in years past, is publisher of a group of newspapers in Maine. He broke into his extremely busy schedule to introduce us to the special couples from Maine who helped make our pages come alive!

Hank and Bunny Searls of Gig Harbor, Washington. Another couple featured in the book, Hank is an old friend of Jack's going all the way back to grammar school days in San Francisco. As a best-selling author of novels and screenplays, Hank gave us significant encouragement at a time when this book was only an idea.

Susan and Burt Sweetow of Scottsdale, Arizona. Great friends of ours—in business together and whose story appears in this book. A source of outstanding ideas, plus a sounding board for us. Always eager to answer our countless questions regarding each stage of the book, the Sweetows were wonderful!

Sue Guries of Santa Rosa, California. Another good friend of many years, bright, funny and so good natured. We asked Sue to do some special research for us, which she did in spades. She also made contacts in our behalf, pointing us in good directions toward profiles for the book. Her help is greatly appreciated.

The Chambers of Commerce in California, of Palm Springs, Santa Barbara, Goleta, and Mill Valley, plus **the Visitors Center of Carmel,** for helping us locate outstanding couples in business from among their memberships. Although we interrupted their busy schedules, they took the matter very seriously and were extremely cooperative.

Also worthy of hearty applause and thanks for their valuable efforts in our behalf are **Sandra Ohlman of Wheaton, IL; Bette Kinsella of Ashland, OR; Alva Manning of Belvedere,**

CA; Karen Redmon of Carmel, CA; Bill Wayland of Scottsdale, AZ; Shelby Kuretsky of Madison, WI; Barbara and Ashley Brown of Woodland Hills, CA; Joan and Will Gill and Fran and Les Stein of Scottsdale, AZ; and Doug Gould of Los Altos, CA.

Special notice should be given to **Christine Goodno of the Service Corps of Retired Executives (S.C.O.R.E.) in Washington, DC**, for her cooperation. The experienced business people who man the S.C.O.R.E. offices have much to contribute to small businesses, especially start-ups.

Heroes all, we applaud and thank these stalwart helpers whose efforts meant so much to us!

BACK-WORD
(The Negative Side)

They said "No, it can't be done!"

For years so many couples have vociferously said to us, "We could never, never, never be in business together!" Maybe they couldn't—or shouldn't. It's not for everybody.

How About You?

(Or, if you're already in business together...could it be even better?)

Please read on!

Fore-Word
(The Positive Side)

Being married...in business has worked for us for 18 years. We've profited, had an exciting time and, incidentally, laughed a lot. Most of our ventures have worked; a couple haven't. On balance the 18 years have been profitable for our business and rewarding for our relationship. We're still at it and still loving it!

In this book we present our story as well as the adventures of 44 very interesting couples who are married...in business. Most of them were seeking independence and at the same time greatly desired to work with each other all day, instead of dashing off to separate jobs.

How-To Basics...Real Life Adventures... and Cartoons, Too!

It is our hope that the how-to basics, the real-life adventures, flavored by the humorous cartoons presented in this book will become part of your research. Of course, only you can determine if it's right for you to be married...in business. Only you can make it work!

We Hope You'll Read and Heed Our **Musts**

In chapter one we present what we're calling our *"musts."* In reality they are vital prerequisites for success in being married...in business. The rest of the book shows these points in action, with practical examples from the real world.

Within the *musts* are individual variables that have only to do with the two of you. Consider these *musts*, think about their implications.

And be sure to *mix **mirth** with your **musts**! Joy is the cement that can keep a business together.*

You Have to Really Want Success!

The purpose of this book is to help you do it—help you to be successfully married…in business, if it's right for you.

So much depends upon *how much* you really want it.

There's a lot to learn, and a lot to accomplish. You'll have to be dedicated, *work smart*, and we believe that it is enormously important to keep your sense of humor—hence the cartooned triflugles (see page 17). Throughout these pages we emphasize that laughter can change your perspective and help carry you through the challenging times.

If you *can* make the grade and be successful together, the rewards can be great! We know, because we've experienced them.

How can you truly know if it's right for you? Only you can decide, and, as we stated, only both of you can make it happen.

We recommend that you clearly face up to the issues we're addressing, digest them (and all of their implications), then plunge into the book with a wide open affirmative attitude.

Read and enjoy, be inspired and maybe, if it's right for you and your spouse, give each other some hugs and kisses, go out for a nice dinner together and then carefully start the oh-so necessary research that MUST be done.

Keep your eyes and ears open, don't rationalize away potential problems—and pray!

Doug and Dot Comm and their Dog, Rom™

© J&E Wyman 1999 World Rights Reserved

The Breakfast Table

A Word About Triflugles

Occasionally we mention *triflugles*. What's a triflugle? Don't bother to look it up in the dictionary; it's our own coined word.

During our years in business together we've made our share of mistakes. This is true of most of the couples interviewed in this book. Some mistakes were minor, some very funny, some even outrageous. The funniest and most outrageous we call "triflugles."

To highlight these triflugles, we've built most of our cartoons around them. We hope you enjoy them.

We wish you many happy days and not too many triflugles—although viewed with perspective, a few triflugles can brighten an otherwise dull day.

About Our Cartoons and Our Cartoonist

By now you've gathered that we think a sense of humor becomes the saving grace for couples in business together. It surely is for us! Desiring to make this book a pleasant read and wanting to give you some chuckles, we hit upon an idea to work with one of the nicest chaps (and one of the best cartoonists in America): Linus Maurer. We've worked with Linus many times over the years in our advertising business, and it's always been an outstanding experience. And now, once again, we've collaborated. We're excited about the results and we hope you will be, too.

Charles Schulz borrowed Linus's name for his famous comic strip, *Peanuts*. Many years ago, Linus and Mr. Schulz worked together as cartoon instructors. And Linus is a *Linus!* He's fun to work with, and he's awfully good! Residing and having his studio in the beautiful California wine country town of Kenwood, Linus is a busy artist. He's received national awards for his humorous graphics, plus he was awarded a top editorial cartoonist award for 1990 by the California Newspaper Publishers Association. Currently Linus produces an international daily syndicated newspaper puzzle, *Challenger,* distributed by King Features.

Linus and Jack are a proven creative team. Together they collaborated to bring you the 41 cartoons that relate to and liven up the book. We think the cartoons help make our points and, at the same time, we hope they give you some merry moments.

Part I
Married...In Business Basics

Chapter One: The Musts

We'll begin with fundamental basics, our ***Musts*** for being successfully married...in business.

The Two of You Should Be Able to Say:

1. **We truly love and respect each other.**
2. **We're each other's best friend.**
3. **We love our business. (Well, at least *one* of us does!)**
4. **We easily and freely communicate within a framework of absolute honesty.**
5. **We set goals within an informal (or formal) business plan, regularly updating income and expense projections.**
6. **We have a deep desire to be of service.***
7. **We're strategically planning to earn a profit.***
8. **We're willing to work as hard as necessary, and are good at it.**
9. **We know our business and never stop learning, bringing in a CPA and other expertise when necessary.**
10. **We know which projects call for teaming up and which call for working separately, always subjugating *ego*—there's no competition between us.**
11. **We are resilient—bolstered by an affirmative attitude and a sense of humor—we never run from adversity.**
12. **We're in the right business at the right time.**

*#6 and #7 are the foundation of our own mission statement.

Note: *The extent to which a couple is able to actually live these musts will go a long way in determining whether or not they should be married...in business. If the couple can't be on the same page, they should at least be in the same book!*

Taking Care of the Married... In Business Relationship

Here are a number of tips and considerations that we have found necessary for a healthy married...in business relationship. Some tie in to the musts, others are extras. All have come from our experience and the experiences of our profiled couples.

Successful Couples Subjugate Egos!

Very vital is a relationship that knows no competition with each other, but one that revels in the other's accomplishments. This should be a relationship that includes a natural desire to buoy up the other's morale when a mistake is made and, of course, to always recognize the other's accomplishments when heroic deeds are done! The best thing is to feel supremely happy when the other one scores a coup and, at the same time, help your partner not to feel badly when he or she makes a poor business decision or a costly mistake.

"Never Talk Business in Bed!"

That's a quote from two of the featured stars of this book, Paul and Sarah Edwards, renowned leaders in the home-based business movement. They should know: The Edwards have been working together for over 20 years.

According to so many couples married...in business, they're right. Maybe not about this specific, but in the general sense. A married couple in business together needs to learn the little things about their relationship that can so easily turn into problems.

In our case, we've found that we should never talk business late at night when we're tired. For us the early morning hours can be pretty good, except for Jack's enthusiastic wake-up big idea that Elaine really doesn't care about until she has both eyes open.

Doug and Dot Comm and their Dog, Rom™

© J&E Wyman 1999 World Rights Reserved

Egos Require Subjugation

What we have found to be true in all relationships is never, never go to bed angry. One party simply must be the one to forget about saving face and be the peacemaker (and do it before it gets too late at night).

Incidentally, here is a very special word of warning: If you're planning to go into business with your spouse be very sure that your temperaments mostly mesh and rarely clash. Okay, we admit that some clashing is inevitable and can be healthy if the clashes avoid bitterness. If there's enough love and respect between the two of you, all will be well. Try to keep those clashes as unemotional as possible and get over them quickly.

Include the Children

Nothing is more important than the well-being of your children. If you have your own home-based business and young children are at home, there are, of course, many benefits available to your family. It's immediately obvious that it will be possible for you to spend more time with the children. However, it will take balancing, including dividing up the duties.

In many instances, people feel that it is easier to concentrate on business with an outside office—securing proper childcare. This point is very individual but must be considered.

We believe that bringing the children into suitable aspects of your business can be of great value to them. If there are business problems to solve, it can be very healthy to inform them, though always in a positive manner. Let them be a part of the family pulling together to the benefit of all, particularly if a problem period means you can't spend money on them the way their friends' parents may be doing. Let the children understand that some sacrifices now can lead to great rewards later, when victory comes.

Even just hearing dinner table business talk can teach the children a great deal. Avoid being negative or sad about the problems. Teach them your CAN-DO attitude (see pages 31-32).

Incidentally, both of us grew up in families (2,000 miles apart) where the total conversation at the table was about the family business. And it didn't hurt us at all. We hope you'll joyously find your own individual way to deal with the balancing act to which we referred.

Communicate, Communicate, Communicate

In the real estate business, the three most important factors for a successful sale are "location, location, location." For couples in business they are "communicate, communicate, communicate."

Communication fits inside of a couple of our *musts*, namely, *truly loving each other*, and *being best friends*. Even if one person is quieter than the other and tends to be less communicative (as in our case), if there is sufficient love and understanding, this can be worked out.

Always Remember to Laugh—A Lot

Not only will your sense of humor help both of you retain a balanced perspective, it's delightful, habit-forming, feels good, and good for you!

Taking Care of the Married... In Business Business

Here are very personal tips and pointers based on our own many years of experience operating a successful entrepreneurial venture.

Doug and Dot Comm and their Dog, Rom™

© J&E Wyman 1999 World Rights Reserved

Communication, Communication, Communication

The Two of You **Are** the Good Business!

Much more significant than your physical headquarters, your logo, your equipment, your college degrees, or any other trapping, it's what's within you that counts! *It's what you have to give.* We believe that it's a matter of how to *benefit* everyone who comes in contact with your business. This means, benefitting each other, staff members, vendors, your customers and, yes, mankind in general.

For *good* business, you should stand for something *good.* You should, of course, be *good* at what you do. You should deeply desire to be productive and, wonder of wonders, the two of you do all of this *together*! And you should have fun doing it!

Work Ethic, Experience and a Good Business Climate

We believe that if you love it, you'll be very willing to make the necessary sacrifices for the good of the business. Of course, that means you should choose a business that you can love.

What about experience in the specific field? Naturally, it's a plus to have either *actual* or *related* experience—or at least to have shown a strong proclivity to adapt to it. That's where the need to keep up the learning process comes in.

Having a favorable business climate, plus positive industry trends are also important. However, if sudden turns in the business climate come about, a CAN-DO attitude helps a lot (see page 31-32).

Research, Research, Research

Before you start your business together do all the research you can. Get advice from informed experts, and from knowledgeable friends and relatives who know you inside and out, who will level with you. Bring your CPA and lawyer into the picture. Talk to others in the same or related businesses. Check out all available information dealing with trends in your field, including the government printing office. Meet with people who work for trade publications in your field and enlist their thinking. If after all of that the lights are green, keep moving forward. Research and understand your *competitive position*. Can you establish your business's unique place in its marketing picture?

Your Mission Statement

Every business needs a mission, an underlying purpose. Get yours going right now. (Preferably written, but—written or not—understood, honored and lived with!) The mission statement can be your business's life-preserver if you hang onto it through thick and thin. It can keep your thinking on the right path.

Our own mission statement is built around two basic ideas: ***have a burning desire to be of genuine, meaningful service; and, at the same time, earn a proper profit***. It's as simple as that, but so vital. If we find ourselves drifting off track or if things aren't going too well, we return to our mission statement. It really defines our business.

We are convinced that a mere desire to make money isn't enough. If it's the only goal, it tends toward greed. However, by strongly desiring to provide a *true service to your market* (and to everyone who is involved with your business), you are fulfilling a meaningful mission, one that will result in your business counting for something. This all-out desire to serve *plus* planning to earn a proper profit is a complete equation.

About Profit

As you know, *profit* is your net after all expenses. It's operating profitably that enables you to pay your vendors and suppliers, *on time*, and to always make your payroll, *on time*. It also allows you to grow the business, and yes, to reward the owners (the two of you) with a proper return on investment.

Doug and Dot Comm and their Dog, Rom™

© J&E Wyman 1999 World Rights Reserved

The Mission Statement

That's right, as soon as the business can afford it (but not before) a definite salary should be part of your fixed expenses. Your income and expense projections will let you know when the time is right.

Be aware that there may be periods when you won't be able to draw a salary. A number of the couples we interviewed made the point that a husband and wife who are planning to go into business together should have adequate personal funds. This is vital to enable them to sustain themselves during the early periods of the business, when it usually can't afford to pay a salary. Be positive that your personal family expenses are in line to be able to survive those non-salaried times. Be ready to make the necessary sacrifices, such as curtailing personal and family costly activities. The ultimate potential rewards far outweigh the sacrifices!

Incidentally, we don't consider *profit* a nasty word. Some have defined it as a *report card* that lets you know how you're managing your business. However, we'd ask that you always keep uppermost in your thinking that *burning desire to be of service.*

Develop a Business Plan

Whether or not you eventually bring investors or a bank into your financing plans, you should have at least a simply stated business plan that evolves into goals. This business plan should be built around income and expense projections. We have found that there's nothing more important for the health of our business than goal-setting, which requires a plan.

"**Set goals and beat them!**" should be your CAN-DO words.

Incidentally, update the projections portion of the business plan at least quarterly. (In our business, we update monthly.)

Organize To Grow

Get advice from your CPA as to the best type of organization and bookkeeping system for you. We advise incorporation as soon as possible, but your CPA should advise you as to the best type of corporation for you.

When we formed our original advertising agency, we operated as a partnership, but set up an accrual bookkeeping system right from the start, just as if we were a large business. Since it seemed to be a professional step, we soon incorporated. We were then able to start a plan for key staff members to purchase stock and become owners in the organization.

After selling that business and now working on a much smaller basis, we are again organized as a corporation, with the two of us the only stockholders. And now we are the only employees, aided by a few very able and creative outside contractors.

Market, Market, Market

How will you bring potential customers to your business? When you did your research you found out everything you could about positioning your business. You determined your "unique selling proposition" in terms of your competition. You found your very own niche.

Now you need to give your customers meaningful reasons to come to you. Create attention-getting advertising that clearly spells out the benefits of your products or services to your market. Make use of all avenues of appropriate public relations and publicity, but do it right. Get outside help if you need it. Create and produce collateral materials that detail your story in your own individual way. Maintain a consistent graphic *family* look in all of your promotional materials.

A Gnawing Need: The Learning Process

Never stop learning about all aspects of your business. Gobble up all the information that you can find from good business publications and newsletters in your field. Get to know trade journal editors and advertising representatives. They can keep you up to date and help you in so many ways.

Join appropriate trade associations, go to seminars and trade shows. Meet and visit with others in the same or similar businesses. Keep up on new developments.

And be sure to let your thinking soar. Be open to new ideas, better ways to serve your customers. The two of you should ask yourselves continually, "What aren't we doing for our customers that we should be doing? How can we be of better service to them?"

Take this learning to the personal level as well. Strive to understand your proven capabilities as well as your potentials. Are the two of you aware of your short-comings that need to be improved? Discuss these and work on ways to improve or eliminate them.

The Can-Do Attitude

Often problems, such as finding that one's business is suffering from having insufficient clout, plus the impact of a negative *business climate*, seem to be out of one's control. We have seen businesses overcome these problems by having the proper, all-out affirmative CAN-DO attitude. This is a state of mind that is always open to new ideas!

We're not advocating mere bravado that becomes unintelligent when external conditions show signs of being permanently adverse. Always face the problem and know when *not* to hang on. However, prior to extreme action, we've found the following philosophy very meaningful:

The Can-Do Attitude Can Cut Through!

To illustrate this, here are three different attitudes. Which one will you choose?

1. ***Little*** **people think in terms of** ***people.*** **("It's** ***who*** **I know that counts. And I don't know the right people!")**
2. ***Medium*** **people think in terms of** ***events.*** **("It's** ***what's going on with the economy or politics*** **that counts. The politicians are hurting my business. And I can't do anything about it!")**
3. ***Big*** **people think in terms of** ***ideas.*** **("I know that** ***fresh, new ideas*** **can lift my business out of the doldrums and enable me to better serve my customers—perhaps in** ***brand new ways!*****")**

Example number three has been our secret for overcoming the problems of not having personal clout and/or experiencing negative external factors. That's the CAN-DO attitude at work!

Doug and Dot Comm and their Dog, Rom™

HIS:

- LAND NEW CLIENTS
- PROFIT BY 1 YEAR
- PLOW BACK PROFITS FOR 3 YEARS
- INCREASE SALARIES EACH YEAR
- OPEN NEW BRANCH BY 3 YEARS

HERS:

- GET HIM TO BUY A NEW SUIT

© J&E Wyman 1999 World Rights Reserved

Goal Setting is Vital

Where To Locate

You will note that nearly all of the couples we interviewed are located in attractive, generally small communities, many near larger cities. We have found that while thousands of couples are certainly successful in big cities, these smaller communities particularly lend themselves to couples in business, both from an economic and desirable lifestyle basis.

Home-Based Or Outside Office-Based?

People ask us, "Does being married...in business relate to businesses that are home-based or outside-office-based?" Our answer: Being married...in business relates to home-based businesses, outside-office-based businesses, or even, no-office-based businesses. *Where* your office is can be vital to you personally, and you should carefully research the subject. By all means, do what suits you best.

We Hope We Haven't Scared You Off!

We're hitting pretty hard at what we think are vital points for success for the couple who wants to be married...in business. Remember at the beginning (in the "Back-word") we stated that working together is not for every couple. We want to give you an idea of what it takes, and for those who are suited to it, it can be wonderful! On the other hand, if you do feel unsure, be grateful to find this out now!

We hope you'll feel comfortable about moving forward. Remember, it might not be easy, and there will be many challenges, but your ultimate victories will be worth it!

Doug and Dot Comm and their Dog, Rom™

© J&E Wyman 1999 World Rights Reserved

Lost and Found Department

Chapter Two: The New Adventure Starts

Getting Married...In Business

Our married...in business career together began in 1980, almost immediately following the start of our extremely happy marriage.

Previously, we had both been single-ized, raised our children, (Elaine's, Sandy and Barbara—and Jack's, Gary, John, Richard and JoAnn), become reasonably happy on our own—and then we met (at church) and—that was it! We fell in love and now, 18 years later, we feel the same way about each other! We truly enjoy being together, and what better way is there to insure that than to be in business together!

We settled in the San Francisco Bay area's Marin County. Elaine had just completed ten years of good business experience with a large San Francisco firm. And Jack continued to direct the busy, medium-sized advertising agency he had founded in San Francisco, with a branch office in Los Angeles.

The advertising business was exciting and challenging, with more than its share of both high and low moments. Through the years we learned that resiliency (see our musts in chapter one) would take care of the low points.

When problems hit we learned to grit our teeth, take some deep breaths, expunge all anger and hurt feelings and start over again! And as for the high points, there's nothing more satisfying than knowing you've solved a client's marketing problem with creative ideas.

Be assured that when we teamed up in business together, we knew we would receive our fair share of both high and low moments. And we have had them. But now we also had each other with whom to share these moments. What a difference that has made!

Turning a Business Around

No sooner had we married and become settled in our new Marin home when the business suddenly slipped into a tenuous situation. Our bookkeeper had been ill and official monthly book closings had been held up, something no business can put up with. (Entrepreneurs please note!) Jack was generally aware that problems had been developing with some of our clientele and our personnel, but it happened so fast he was shocked when updated figures were finally presented to him. The company had just moved from San Francisco to Mill Valley, the move being a major, all-absorbing (horrible) activity. And Jack was also very caught up with the excitement of his coming marriage.

Over the years the company had experienced only one bad year, but that one was a doozy. It was largely the result of an acquisition arrangement with another advertising agency that didn't work out, as well as the loss of the agency's largest client due to a major management change.

In order to keep functioning, the agency needed additional working capital to make up for the large loss. Jack worked up projections that showed any bank how a sizable loan would be repaid out of new projected profits. (**IMPORTANT NOTE**: To operate soundly, a firm must always pay back a loan out of profits.)

Jack approached a few banks, but found it amusing that some of the very banks that had solicited his business during the many years when he didn't need a loan were pretty aloof now

Doug and Dot Comm and their Dog, Rom™

© J&E Wyman 1999 World Rights Reserved

Entering Politics

that he needed one. The agency's track record plus Jack's projections saved the day and he acquired a five-year, $50,000 loan. (The year was 1971; the equivalent dollar value of the loan would be many times that figure, today.) The agency went through some minor downsizing, stepped up it's sales effort, landed the largest client it had ever worked with, and paid the loan back in two years. (A number of those interviewed for this book proudly told us how they were able to pay off their loans very quickly, well before they were due.) Never again was any significant financing necessary.

Now, nine years later, due to the bookkeeper's illness, the move, plus the excitement of our wedding, things briefly slipped out of control. This occurred just prior to Elaine's joining the business. Shortly after our marriage, Jack phoned home to say that he'd be late for dinner as something had come up at the office. The bookkeeper's closing statement had just been presented to him. The figures showed that we had lost a lot of money in the previous month, and were headed for the same thing in the current month. And the next month looked worse. That's what came up!

Arriving home, Jack presented the sad picture to Elaine, followed by a sigh and the plaintive statement: "Well, we can turn it around, if we want to. We've done it before. The question is, do we want to?"

Almost immediately he followed that question with a strong answer, "Yes, we *do* want to!" And, of course Elaine agreed.

Together At Last!

(Every day, every night, every weekend! *Ain't love (and business) grand?*)

But how will the existing staff react to the boss' wife working with him at the top level of the company?

And so our married…in business adventure began.

Elaine joined the company and took over two duties. Functionally she became the media buyer, which means she bought the time and space in which our clients' ads and commercials appeared. (This she had to learn and master, which she did.) Her other—and most significant—job was in management, working with Jack to administer and guide a much-needed downsizing of the business.

First she researched out any and all profit leaks. (Not the choicest first job for the new top management person to tackle.) This meant scrutinizing company and personal staff expenses and examining cost-accounting records to determine profitability of clients, with particular emphasis on account executive profitability. It also meant looking closely at the costs of creative personnel, plus an analysis of the need for the Los Angeles office.

We carefully examined Elaine's findings, and then came the tough part. We let a number of people go, closed the Los Angeles office, cut executive salaries and resigned unprofitable clients.

At the same time, we launched an active new business sales drive, which led to exciting days and nights of working very hard preparing sales presentations, with extremely satisfying results. We ended up gradually building an effective, dedicated staff serving the best of our old clients plus interesting, valuable new ones.

And can you guess what happened? We rescued the current year, so that there was only a bare minimum loss, but best of all, the business *turned around*, and what followed were the two most profitable bottom-line years in the history of the business. All led by the two of us, married...in business!

Let's pause for a minute and look back at some high points of this period.

Now a Husband and Wife Are in Charge

And Strange Things Begin to Happen

Now, we must tell you about some of the unique, noteworthy and funny experiences we had as a husband and wife operating the business during the turn-around period.

With Elaine's first assignment to research and find profit leaks, she uncovered some interesting information. Of all things, people were using the company phones to make frequent personal long-distance calls. And not just little quickies either. As this came to light, a horrified Elaine had to confront and stop the defensive and embarrassed perpetrators.

The Complaint About the New Management

People who didn't know it soon found out that Elaine had Jack's total support. Once a young, cocky, but very good account executive came into Jack's office, closed the door and complained about Elaine. It seems that a very attractive young woman on the staff, who had been properly corrected by Elaine for whatever reason, had complained to the account executive. And here he was complaining about Elaine to Jack.

The account executive said, "Jack, Elaine has got to stop ragging on Mary (not her name); I don't want her to quit!"

Jack said, "Do you realize that you're complaining about our executive vice-president, who also happens to be my wife?" Then Jack followed with some well chosen words such as, "Elaine has my complete support. She's doing the job she was brought in to do, and she's doing it right!" End of meeting. End of problem.

Husbands and wives in business together do have to face such issues and be ready for them.

Jack's Call for Help!

A new, very efficient secretary had virtually refused to follow the agency's traditional formats and ways of presenting information. Every single assignment given to her by Jack came back in a different form. This went on for some time, with Jack pleading for her to present the material in the form he requested.

One morning the secretary went too far. Jack had gone to the outer office to pick up her typed material. And, once again she did it the way she wanted it, which was not the way he wanted it. She vigorously refused to change it and proceeded to let Jack know he was wrong.

Jack was totally frustrated. Not wanting a scene in the outer office, but completely unable to cope without answering the woman in kind, he yelled at the top of his voice, "ELAINE, COME OUT HERE!" and walked away. Now, there's a *triflugle*!

A startled Elaine properly handled the situation, and with mutual agreement, the secretary left at once (permanently.)

The Excess Furniture Problem

Here's another one that Elaine will never let Jack forget

(This should interest you if you ever have to move your office into a smaller space, such as moving into a home-based business office.)

Yes, Elaine put up with a lot when she first started to run the company with Jack. As stated, the office had just been moved to Mill Valley from San Francisco. We had occupied larger offices in San Francisco, and Jack had given instructions to the staff member in charge of the move to get rid of excess furniture and anything else that wasn't needed. He told him, "If in doubt, *throw it out!"*

However, the very overly-conscientious gentleman just couldn't. The result: An enormous amount of excess furniture and equipment was delivered to the new office, jamming walkways and aisles, a mess. Actually, the gentleman retired just prior to the move and never even showed up at the new office, with its overflowing furniture.

On this particular morning (one of Elaine's first on the job), Jack came to Elaine's office and told her that a very important client was coming to the office the next morning for a major meeting. He then desperately said, "We've just got to get rid of that mountain of extra furniture and stuff, before the client gets here."

Elaine said, "But how?"

Jack answered, "I don't know, but just get rid of it. I'm going out for a cup of coffee!" And he left. A bewildered Elaine called a nearby used furniture store and, with a lot of pleading, managed to have the excess furniture picked up that afternoon.

You may be sure that the two of us still laugh about that situation. Rightfully, Jack will never hear the end of it. A definite, king-sized *triflugle*!

"I'm going out for a cup of coffee," indeed!

Eliminating Unprofitability

In order for a business to turn around usually two things have to be done. One is cut expenses. The other is increase sales. In our business, salaries represented over 60 percent of total expenses. It's easy to see that cutting staff always seemed the first step in cutting expenses.

However, that's very difficult to do. First there's the personal relationship problem. You don't want to hurt people. It was always a dreadful feeling for us to realize upon arising on a given morning that we were going to have to cut somebody from the staff that day. It's a terrible ordeal to go through, the hardest thing for management to face.

Further, if you eventually expect business to pick up, you'll be looking to hire again. And that means you'll very likely have to train new people all over again. A very challenging problem.

Doug and Dot Comm and their Dog, Rom™

© J&E Wyman 1999 World Rights Reserved

The Computer is Down

In any event, you especially don't want to drop anybody who has been doing a good job. Nevertheless, there are times that the cutting of staff simply has to be accomplished if a business is to survive.

We always knew that it was better to cut staff than to have the entire business go under. Good management simply has to be able to face these situations and have the courage and fortitude to carry out the right action.

Over the years we learned one very heartening thing. If a person no longer belonged in our organization (or if we simply couldn't afford the individual), we made a terrible mistake if we thought that *we* were the person's only hope.

We believe that each individual has very wonderful things to offer in the right situation. We learned that, actually, we could be preventing the person from finding his or her right place if we kept the person on. We have seen this happen more than once. It's a truism.

Nevertheless, we always made every effort to minimize staff cuts, yet the turn-around we currently faced demanded it.

One significant expense-cutting step during challenging times has been cutting key people's salaries—especially our own. We've found that our truly loyal people were willing to have their salaries cut rather than to have to leave the company. What a joy it is to return these salaries to their normal level when business picks up!

A Special No-No: Unprofitable Clients

In our case we took an additional step. Our cost accounting numbers showed that we had been carrying some unprofitable clients—clients who demanded too much service for the revenue that they developed.

In one instance Elaine met with a very able account executive who handled more than one account that fit this category. One of his clients, particularly, was costing us a great deal of money (travel expenses, staff time, etc.) while developing very little in the way of income. Upon being questioned about this, the account executive told Elaine that if we did anything to shake up the client, such as cutting back on our service or charging more, many ad agencies would hear of this and flock to this client seeking his business and we'd lose the account.

To us this was a point of view that would lead to a gigantic triflugle. Elaine said, "Well, why not let them have the account? Why do we want it if it's unprofitable?" The account executive, so imbued with the prestige of handling this client, couldn't understand Elaine's position.

Note: We eventually parted company with both this account executive and his unprofitable clients. He was a very able, likable advertising man and went into business for himself. Probably, on his own, with very little overhead, he was able to profitably handle his business.

That's a case in point. By letting the account executive go, we freed him to find his right direction, keep his clients, and undoubtedly become a happier, more successful person. And we remained friends, too!

The other part of the turn-around equation is new sales. And we went after it! We landed two major financial institutions, one of which was very prestigious and also developed significant income for our company.

So the turn-around happened and we saved the current year by showing a minuscule loss, but we were now geared to truly move ahead full force. We hired some very bright young people, one a young copywriter who was so eager to join us that, at his own speculation, he developed a fine radio campaign for one of our clients. We hired him, raised him and raised him, but finally lost him to a much larger ad agency in San Francisco. Eventually, he went to a major national agency in New York, where his abilities allowed him to work on huge national accounts.

As for us, we then proceeded to enjoy the best bottom-line years in the history of our business.

Following these events, we decided it was time for us to have a whole new experience. We sold our business to three key employees and moved to Scottsdale, Arizona, to find new adventures.

Off To Scottsdale!

In 1983, at the time we sold our original advertising agency, the business was operating very profitably. We remained available for consultation even though we moved to Arizona.

Our plan was to try part-time retirement and, at the same time, enter a whole new world from a geographical and business standpoint. We hoped we would find our way back into, at least, a satisfying part-time business together. Happily, we did!

Our first effort was to organize a consulting group made of up retired executives. We figured that companies might be relieved to hire the thinking of seasoned veterans—from their field—who would work on a part-time basis for them. The idea had a lot of merit and Jack did receive a number of consulting jobs, one of which lasted about ten years.

However, Jack had to do his consulting under his own auspices because the group that we established had ideas that caused us to withdraw from it. The group drifted into a milieu of not wanting to work in the fields from which the consultants had retired. They wanted to spend their efforts trying to find financing for companies that needed it. All well and good, but not for us. We sold out of the group at a small loss, but it was worth it.

We learned that at this point in our careers, we definitely preferred to function as a two-person, husband-and-wife team, married...in business. After buying out our covenant-not-to-compete with the people to whom we sold our advertising agency, we went back into advertising in a very small and selective manner. And now virtually all of our efforts are in writing and publishing.

Our first book together came out in 1994 and is entitled, *Retired? Get Back in the Game!* We learned a great deal, had a wonderful time, researching, writing and publishing the book, which found its way across the country. This experience led to the book you are now reading, though this book is for all age groups, from junior to senior.

Reviewing the Musts that Came to Life in the Foregoing Adventures

1. We were motivated by true love and respect for each other. We owed it to each other to conquer the immediate challenge. We called forth an already deeply ingrained resiliency that refused to run away from the problem. We had a great desire and determination to turn the business around and experience the joy of an ultimate return to profitability. And we did it!

2. The fact that we were (and are) best friends made the time spent in working together a delight. We laughed a great deal, seeing humor in so many things that happened—usually at our own expense. We found that *joy is indeed the cement that holds a business together!*

3. We communicated and communicated and communicated, at any time and any place!

4. Jack indefatigably worked on updated income and expense projections, which were the basis of our goals. The projections truly became goal projections. When he shared these projections with other key people (which wasn't often), they were very skeptical that the desired figures could be realized. But they were indeed attained—and surpassed.

5. Jack's long experience and Elaine's sound thinking meant that *we knew our business.*

These and many more *musts* continue to come into play during our married...in business challenge.

PART II
Married...In Business Profiles

Meet The Stars

Now, meet the real stars of this book, the 44 couples whom we had the delightful experience of interviewing.

What to Look for While You Are Reading

1. Entrepreneurial Ideas: Each couple's story leads off with the type of business, followed by the name of the firm. This information can be a quick source of entrepreneurial ideas.

2. The People: Next you'll find the names of the principals that we are proud to present to you. They represent a group of some of the finest, most able—and often humorous—people we've ever met. We've been enriched by getting to know them. We think you will be, too!

3. The Places: Next you'll see the names of the often unique cities and towns in which our couples operate their businesses. There is an enormous horizon open to most couples thinking of being married…in business. Research it for yourselves and find the area that measures up to what you've always wanted. It could greatly enhance your chosen business and home experience.

4. The Interviews: Next come the results of our interviews: brief looks at each business and the couple operating it. The stories are peppered with incidents, strategy, challenges and some laughs, too. Most share their philosophies in telling how they make their partnership work, and many give advice to other couples who may be considering going into business together.

Getting Into the Business

One of the most significant and inspiring areas of interest in the stories that follow is *how* each couple went into their specific business. Look for these three ways:

1. The couple very creatively analyzed a skill that one or both had developed while working for another company. They saw bigger possibilities with the skill, tweaked it a bit and turned it into a brand new business. On occasion the move into an independent operation came with the blessing of the former company. A variation of this is the situation where a person's hobby became an independent business. In any event, we consider this category "Creatively adapting a former skill into a new independent business."

2. The couple purchased an existing business. Either by contacting a business broker or by responding to a business opportunity ad, the couple got in touch with the business they eventually purchased. Here is where our point about thorough research comes into distinct focus. We emphasize that this situation (like the others) demands the right attitude for going into the venture. Don't think it will be easier.

3. One or both the husband or wife had special training, such as advanced schooling or a supervised apprenticeship on the job. Eventually the couple took that training and established their own independent business together.

Motivation

Virtually every couple whose experience is about to be told wanted to be in business together for these reasons:

- ✔ **They greatly desired independence and the opportunity to build something that would be good for their future.**
- ✔ **They wanted to be together in business as well as at home. In addition to having love for each other, they were *best* friends.**

Now, we hope you enjoy and are inspired by these stories.

Doug and Dot Comm and their Dog, Rom™

© J&E Wyman 1999 World Rights Reserved

The New Logo

Internet Providers

Impulse Internet Services

Ken and Lena Alker
Santa Barbara, California

(Epitomize creativity...ideas become profit centers...workaholics...needed an Internet provider for their specialized needs—launched their own...now 4,000 subscribers...problem solvers)

As an electrical and computer engineer working for other companies, Ken Alker was such an idea man that it was a foregone conclusion that he'd eventually have his own business. Ken's constant flow of fresh ideas always seemed to have practical applications that led to profits, so it had to happen.

He broke the ice as a part-time independent consultant while still working for a local engineering firm. His consulting work soon grew so that he resigned his job to consult full-time.

Ken's wife, Lena, soon also left a good position to join him, together forming Impulse Engineering. She learned and mastered circuit board design and developed her own customer base.

However, it wasn't long before Ken had another idea that took off and became a profitable venture. The result: They formed a second company and now have a staff of 12!

Ken and Lena, now married 11 years, are an unusually bright, all-out problem-solving, hard-working couple. In fact they admit to being workaholics.

The Alkers have two children, 9 and 11, who are virtually growing up with the business in a family-oriented atmosphere. Not surprisingly, both children are computer literate.

Back to Ken's idea that has evolved into a very stimulating business. Like millions of others around the nation, Ken and Lena found themselves requiring Internet access for their engineering business. But they wanted features that the large servers just couldn't provide. So Ken decided that they should start their own Internet access business and offer it to Santa Barbara and the surrounding areas, which include Lompoc, Santa Maria, the Santa Ynez Valley and Santa Barbara itself. As he thought it through and began his research, Ken realized that indeed a small server could do a good job for individuals and businesses who wanted their special needs to be considered.

The Alkers started out with a very modest investment. This was made possible by purchasing used equipment. They set up 100 modems in each of their four locations. Initially the Alkers actually made cables themselves. Now successful, upgrading their equipment is an on-going activity.

It was a standing, very economical start, but the idea was right, the work ethic the best and the technical engineering knowledge, superior.

The Alkers now have over 500 modems and 4,000 subscribers, whom Ken states never have to put up with a busy signal when they sign-on to their server. Customer service is available extended hours and phones are manned by a friendly and helpful staff.

As for their division of duties, Ken currently spends much of his time upgrading facilities from analog to digital. He also actively seeks suitable acquisitions, and is in charge of integrating an acquired firm into the expanding company. Ken is also responsible for accounts payable and for most bookkeeping duties.

Lena handles all personnel matters and supervises customer service, fields customer billing concerns and, in general, acts as the communications hub for the busy company. Their growing staff has gradually moved into a number of these activities.

Ken and Lena have a very obviously supportive relationship. Lena is more conservative than Ken and admits that sometimes his ideas seem overly adventurous at first glance. However, she knows, trusts and supports his history in making his ideas successful. Lena continues to love the challenges that are presented to her. One suspects that this will go on for a long time!

The story of the Alkers should be an inspiration to couples all over the nation. Their experience vividly shows how one husband and wife team can start as a very small business and eventually establish their own niche in today's exploding computer industry. Theirs is an example of the power of an idea, introduced at the right time, backed by the necessary knowledge and an all-out work ethic.

(www.impulse.net)

Doug and Dot Comm and their Dog, Rom™

© J&E Wyman 1999 World Rights Reserved

The Long Range Marketing Plan

NOVELTIES
FANCY BANDS-Garters

Custom Accessories
Ward and Nancy Swenson
Theresa, Wisconsin

(She had a fresh idea...created samples...he called on stores, took orders...an expanding business was born...no single boss...have individual domains...she designs, he sells... settle differences quickly)

Here's a true entrepreneurial story that is worthy of an award for originality. Let's set the stage:

Located in Theresa, Wisconsin, Ward and Nancy Swenson, who were married in 1990, had totally different occupational experiences. Earlier in his career, Ward had been a popular television and radio weatherman. After leaving the world of broadcasting, he experienced one disappointing business venture and was a bit leery of starting another.

Nancy had worked as a floral designer in a flower shop for 16 years. It was here that an interesting idea hit her. Gradually it advanced from "what if?" to "why not?" and eventually to "let's try it!"

For some time, high-schoolers had been bringing garters to the floral shop to be decorated for their proms. Nancy, observing this trend, felt maybe she and Ward could turn the idea into a going business.

Somewhat reluctant at first, Ward agreed, figuring that since he was retired, Nancy's idea might provide some good activity for him. Ward said that if Nancy would make them, he'd sell them. At the beginning, Ward took Nancy's decorated samples to a few stores in Milwaukee and easily sold 20. Next, Carson, Pirie, Scott & Co. picked up garters for their 50 stores.

At this point Nancy resigned her job at the florist and began making garters full time.

The next major chain to order the Swenson's Fancy Bands garters was Things Remembered, for 50 of their stores. A number of these stores primarily dealt with engraving, so when the high school students came in to purchase garters, they could also get a charm and have it individually engraved with name and date.

In 1996 the couple began selling to bridal shops nationwide by way of Ward's efforts on the telephone. Next they created a 40-page catalog that presented 160 styles.

Nancy designs the garters using black, white and ivory lace. She's also developed sports garters called Fan Bands—for fans of all professional sports teams but especially followers of the Green Bay Packers. Since these bands are not licensed by the teams, the Swensons use the appropriate colors but not the logos. They also have bands for high school basketball, baseball and soccer teams, as well as individualized arm bands and garters for cheerleaders. These are decorated with gold or silver stamped ribbons and include football or basketball charms. Soon the couple were prompted to add Biker Bands—black and orange head bands with a hog embossed on the band.

After Nancy designs the bands, both use the very large, heavy duty sewing machine. Ward feeds the material into the machine and Nancy catches it. She hand sews the small decorations to the garters and can turn out between 6 to 15 an hour after the material is serged.

The solid way the Swensons do business is evidenced by the purchase of their large sewing machine. Ward went to the bank with $15,000 worth of orders in hand. He easily secured the loan and financed the machine. They paid off the loan in ten days.

Interestingly, Ward and Nancy do no other advertising than on their Website. Most of their selling now results from sending out samples, which Ward follows up on with a phone call.

As for Ward and Nancy's married…in business relationship, no one is the *boss*. Each of their areas of expertise are clearly defined. If there are any differences of opinions, they're quickly resolved.

The couple's office and production facilities are in their home, with Nancy's design and sewing operations located on the second floor. Ward does his phoning and faxing from his separate office downstairs, so the couple don't have a great deal of contact during the day.

Both of the Swensons feel that long ago they served their business apprenticeship as employees. Now they're delighted to have the product and the know-how to design, produce and sell their idea, which is being enthusiastically accepted on a national basis.

Ward and Nancy Swenson and their Fancy Bands garters should be an inspiration to all budding entrepreneurs. They've shown the power of a creative idea put into action in a practical manner—and with a lot of gusto!

(www.garters.com)

Doug and Dot Comm and their Dog, Rom™

© J&E Wyman 1999 World Rights Reserved

The Bath

LANDSCAPE CONSTRUCTION

(Bocce Ball Court Installation)

Boccebrew

David and Sandy Brewer
San Rafael, California

(New idea turned past experience into new industry...diverse talents merged into the new company...some disagreements inevitable...give each enough room...home-based office begets paper-creep)

Here's a story that should give hope to all who dream of someday discovering a new idea that can open up new avenues of success.

David Brewer of San Rafael, California, went into the landscape construction business with a partner in 1978. Ten years later, feeling the need for a change, he began to function as a subcontractor.

Dave's wife of 27 years, Sandy, worked as an office manager for an import and export company. She had been working in offices since her teens and had tired of working for others in this manner.

A year-and-a-half ago, Sandy had an idea that the two of them were able to turn into a brand new business. They had been invited to a friend's home where they were captivated by a simple and apparently great game that everybody (including the handicapped) could enjoy. The game is called bocce ball, and it has been around for hundreds of years.

The Brewers had never seen a bocce ball court at someone's home. Then came the hunch that bocce ball courts could be constructed to adapt not only to countless homes, but that businesses, too, might see great advantages in making bocce ball available for employees. For example, a law firm in San Francisco has had a small bocce ball court constructed on their roof, for the relaxation of their attorneys.

The Brewers aren't alone in their enthusiasm! Bocce ball appears to be really catching on. Clubs are being set up, and the movement is growing. There are even plans under consideration to make it an Olympic Games event.

Incidentally, bocce ball is played with a lead ball called a pallino, which is tossed at least halfway down the court. The object of the game is to get one's own ball (about five inches in diameter) closest to the pallino or to strike an opponent's ball away from the pallino. Simple, but great fun!

Dave and Sandy formally teamed up early in 1997 and set up their new business. Their company is called *Boccebrew.*

Though their business background was very diverse, they quickly fused their differing talents into a smooth-running operation. Sandy handles public relations and marketing (she makes initial sales contacts and puts proposals together) and normal administrative functions. Dave designs the bocce ball court as part of the entire area, with patios, plants, and trellises—to the client's individual specifications.

It is interesting to note that the bottom layers of the court are crushed rock packed with a layer of oyster shells mixed with clay and handpacked. Handily, when a court suffers from wear and tear, it requires only to be dragged like a baseball field and then rolled with a lawn roller to return it to playing condition.

As for recommendations to other couples who are considering going into business together, Dave feels that all husbands and wives in business should face the fact that there are bound to be disagreements. He feels that with each partner allowing the other enough room, the disagreements can be easily minimized.

One problem that besets the Brewers, common to all who have home-based businesses, is the "paper creep." While their office is downstairs, their dining room table, which is upstairs, is perpetually covered with papers dealing with their business.

Dave believes in having other interests beyond business. He regularly plays the Flamenco guitar in a musical group, from which he receives much enjoyment. This is a truly creative couple who turned an idea into a business.

Doug and Dot Comm and their Dog, Rom™

© J&E Wyman 1999 World Rights Reserved

Home Office Dress Code

Home-based Business Movement

Leading Authorities on Working from Home: Speakers and Authors

Paul and Sarah Edwards
Santa Monica, California

(Pioneers...epitomize resiliency...innovators... perfectionists...no ego problems...mutually supportive...highly educated in differing fields... found the way to work together at home)

Some of the stories of our couples who are married...in business emphasize the *how-to* aspects of their businesses. In the case of Paul and Sarah Edwards, their exceptionally strong personal relationship is featured.

The Edwards met at the University of Missouri and married a few weeks before graduation. They admit that even then they were love birds who really didn't want to work apart from each other! However, they proceeded to work at their different jobs. Sarah became a licensed psychotherapist, ultimately building a private practice. Paul, after receiving a law degree, conducted a political campaign and public affairs consulting business. But Paul and Sarah didn't like being apart all day. Not at all! They'd ask, "Is this the way it's going to be? Do we have to wait until we're 65 before we can be together all day?"

And so the Edwards found their way. First, they brought each other into the various projects that each happened to be working on in their separate businesses. Then they moved both of their businesses into their home, but continued focusing on their own individual work. This was fortuitous as it kept an income stream going.

Finally, in 1980, Paul and Sarah began writing their first of what is now ten books on the subject of *working from home.* They are indeed leading authorities on the subject.

Soon they began giving commercially sponsored talks and seminars. Today, almost 20 years later, Paul and Sarah still lead exciting lives, traveling for personal appearances, writing, and, quite naturally making many appearances on the media. They've also had their own shows on national radio and television—all on the subject of self-employment and *working from home.*

The Edwards find that their education, especially in psychology, helps them to present meaningful information —particularly for couples working from home. Hearing Paul and Sarah describe their own relationship, married...in business, is refreshing. Here are a few of their very telling comments:

"We truly love being together and working together! We respect the expertise and contribution of the other and are in no way competitive! We never want to outshine the other. We're happiest when the other is happy. If one of us is a bit down, the other tries to bring joy and lightness to the one needing it."

They both agree that *resilience* is the quality that has been their saving grace. They get over a moment of depression by getting right back to work. This is a vital point for all couples in business together.

It's interesting to note that at different times, each is apt to come up with the big idea that makes a difference in their business. This usually happens when they are away from their office with its telephone, paper stacks, and deadlines.

They acknowledge that Sarah is the faster writer. Paul enjoys research and taking time to search out just the right word or phrase that will enhance the passage. Paul says that if the writing were left entirely to him, it wouldn't get finished.

As for vacations, how about once a year—the week between Christmas and New Years. And that's it. But soon they're moving their home office to the mountains where they can walk out the door into the wilderness for an instant vacation. Paul and Sarah Edwards epitomize the complete package of qualities and abilities so needed for a couple's success in business together!

(www.paulandsarah.com)

Doug and Dot Comm and their Dog, Rom™

© J&E Wyman 1999 World Rights Reserved

The Paper Creep

SURVEYING/MAPPING

Maine Coast Surveying
Maine Mapping
Rory and Luci Craib
Damariscotta, Maine

(Two distinct established and growing businesses—operated together...one's his (surveying)... research led to hers (mapping)...very supportive... love outdoors—even to surveying in snowshoes)

Rory and Luci Craib of Damariscotta, Maine are two very bright, very innovative people who have developed two distinct businesses. You might say that they function independently together.

Time has proven that they're in the right businesses and certainly in the right area for their specialized careers and their personal happiness. Both agree enthusiastically that they love the outdoors! Even winter weather, which sometimes requires the donning of snowshoes for their surveying and mapping activities, doesn't slow them down. Not at all.

Married for 24 years, the couple have been teamed up in business for the past nine. Prior to that Rory had been a surveyor working for others, until he made the break to become independent.

Meanwhile Luci had a very fine position working for the federal government for 11 years. She enjoyed her work, which involved a long commute to and from Augusta. Eventually, she was ready for a change.

About that time Rory became very aware that computer technology for mapping, which had been developed 12 years ago, was now coming to the personal computer platform. He and Luci then proceeded to extensively research computer equipment, software and training, feeling that this development could possibly open up a new career for Luci.

And that's exactly what happened. The result of their intensive study is Maine Mapping, which Luci started in 1989.

Even though the Craibs' businesses are separate, their activities are certainly related. The couple share offices in Damariscotta Village, and as would be expected, they discuss their businesses, share ideas and help each other with problems. They are-mutually supportive and work hard at their jobs.

Luci says that it took about five years for her business to really take hold. This was to Luci's liking, because when she started the business, their daughter was very young, and Luci was able to spend considerable time with her—much more than if she had still been working for the government with her long commute to Augusta.

Asked how she acquired clients, starting from ground zero, Luci says that she prepared presentations, gave demonstrations, invited people in to her office, bid on contracts—*ad infinitum.*

And it worked. Finally she began to get some business. Then after five years it became well established. Happily, its success continues.

Much of Luci's business comes from municipalities. She works a great deal on zoning maps, reflecting the need to redo existing maps according to changes in regulations and ordinances. Currently she's doing a lot of mapping for a statewide enhanced 911 project to bring road-maps up to date.

Rory's surveying activities deal primarily with property boundary work. He researches and recovers boundaries for individuals, as well as for commercial clients. His assignments vary from working on a quarter-acre lot in Damariscotta to a 200-acre wooded lot in the hinterlands. Rory's business took between three and four years to become solidly established.

The couple have three full-time people on their staff, two in the field plus one office manager. Finding and training people for their specialized type of work has been difficult, but obviously the Craibs have managed to accomplish this.

Operating frugally, especially as the couple started up their enterprises, they were cautious about the purchase of equipment. Gradually over the years—reflecting their ongoing success—the Craibs have upgraded and acquired what amounts to a sizable investment in equipment.

As for advice to other couples who may be considering going into business together, Rory and Luci say that since the couple will have all their eggs in one basket, they should certainly be sure that they are going into the right kind of work.

They add that the couple must be prepared to work hard, that there will certainly be some discouraging days that they should be ready to work through. The Craibs also recommend that (as continually repeated in this book), the couple should have fun at their work, that they should truly like each other and share common goals.

Rory and Luci Craib of Damariscotta, Maine, are outstanding examples of what they recommend to other couples. In addition they are extremely intelligent surveyors and map-makers who have established an enviable record—one of which they can be proud!

Doug and Dot Comm and their Dog, Rom™

© J&E Wyman 1999 World Rights Reserved

Buying the New Copy Machine

Author (Novelist), Screenwriter, Consultant

Hank Searls Authors' Workshop

Hank and Bunny Searls
Gig Harbor, Washington

(Totally supportive of each other...he writes the books and screen plays, critiques wannabees... she's the sounding board, researcher, editor, computer expert, bookkeeper...true adventurers on land and sea)

An author of best-selling novels, with 19 published books plus countless successful screenplays, should by rights lead an exciting, adventuresome life.

In the case of Hank and Bunny Searls, that's an accurate description of their life together—married...in business! A unique business at that.

Alongside Hank's prolific novel and screenplay writing, plus his critiquing of other authors' works, we find Bunny editing, researching, collaborating, handling the bookkeeping and operating the computer.

Now here's perhaps the most fascinating part: Consider the couple's three-and-a-half year trip on a 40-foot ketch from the West Coast to the South Seas, during which time they lived on the boat at Tahiti for about a year.

Then there was the trip with the two of them on one motorcycle, all the way up the West Coast from San Diego to the Oregon border.

Also, we should note the couple's historically significant researching trip in a motor home. That was the time they accurately followed the journal of Hank's great grandfather who, during the gold rush of the mid-1800s, crossed the country into California. They had the thrill of staying at some of the exact areas where Hank's great grandfather had camped. By now, you're viewing an accurate picture of Hank and Bunny Searls.

To add to their importance to this book, the couple are prime examples of husbands and wives in business together who have moved to fascinating locations. These locations offer them a very desirable lifestyle. They live at Gig Harbor, Washington, a peaceful fishing village located right on beautiful Puget Sound. This is the location they chose, after population growth chased them out of the Malibu and Newport Beach areas of Southern California. They've lived at Gig Harbor for 11 years.

To bring the couple more specifically to life, we'll start with Hank. After graduating from the United States Naval Academy during World War II, Hank became a Navy pilot. While in the Navy he began writing and selling short stories that quite naturally dealt with aviation. He also became involved in Navy film work, which introduced him to the Hollywood studio scene. This set the stage for a writing career when he returned to civilian life.

Soon Hank began to write and sell what became his successful novels and screenplays. His books, *Jaws 2, Overboard, Crowded Sky, Sounding, The New Breed* and *Kataki*, clearly put him in the category of a best-selling author.

Hank and Bunny met when Hank had some business at one of the major Hollywood studios. He happened to go by the set where a scene was being shot for the popular show, *77 Sunset Strip*. Bunny, who had a busy career as a model and actress, was in the scene and was being attacked by one of the leading characters. Hank wanted to jump onto the set and save her. Needless to say they met, married, and here they are 39 years later.

In addition to writing novels and screen plays, the couple has added an additional element to their activities. They have established a writers' workshop for both inexperienced and experienced authors. Hank, with Bunny's editorial assistance, critiques manuscripts and screenplays, then consults one-to-one with the writers. This method gives invaluable insight into how-to-do-it, how-not-to-do it and why.

Their philosophy is that once the writer has actually written an entire manuscript, he or she is in a position to understand and learn what it takes to be successful. Hank feels that this system is much more effective than the classroom method, where students discuss theory first and write later. With the Searls' system, the critique becomes pointedly effective and meaningful.

As for that trip to the South Seas—the couple purchased their ketch in San Francisco. With the two of them as the only crew, they sailed to the South Seas, visiting, among other exotic ports, Bora Bora, Tahiti and New Zealand.

A humorous event took place in Tahiti. It was known in the area that Hank and Bunny were aboard their boat. Not surprisingly, a group of people gathered to watch them. They admit to showing off a bit, trying to look salty as they were pulling on a line. Suddenly, the line gave way and the two of them made rather ungraceful backward swan dives into the water. The onlookers knew that the couple was working on their book, *Overboard*. Very apropos!

To this day, Hank marvels at how Bunny, who had no nautical experience, adapted to life on the ketch. He tells of how she learned enough to take over much of the navigator's duties, to Hank's delight. She asked him to teach her as if it were paint-by-numbers—with no theory thrown in—and it worked!

Their adventures make two important points. First, Hank has written his books from first-hand research. Second, it's very obvious that Hank and Bunny are an outstanding team, a rare couple whose accomplishments together know no limits.

(www.hanksearls-ms-critique.com)

Home Furnishings

MacKenzie-Childs, Ltd.

Victoria and Richard MacKenzie-Childs
Aurora, New York

(From two struggling artists in 1983, to a staff of 400... create fresh designs presenting ideals of joy, loveliness and purity...in spirited furniture, home furnishings, majolica dinnerware, glassware, linen and more... enlightened management)

Here's a spectacular growth story. To observe MacKenzie-Childs, Ltd. today it's hardly imaginable to think that their staff could ever have numbered only two. But it did. Back in 1983 it was just Victoria and Richard MacKenzie-Childs.

Both holding master's degrees in fine art, the couple found themselves primarily designing clothing in a very quiet way. Their work could be called a well-kept secret, except among their circle of friends.

However, a necessity to increase their earnings reared its head. Their daughter, Heather, expressed a strong desire to study ballet in England. And Victoria and Richard were determined to find the way to support their daughter's wishes.

So the couple began to explore their opportunities. Their friends did everything they could to discourage them, saying that they'd never be able to make a success of selling their creative concepts in the commercial marketplace—an attitude that only spurred them on.

The couple certainly could be called struggling artists, but in addition to living with the barest of necessities, their primary struggle went much deeper than all of the external demands. They deeply sought, suffered and listened to find breakthrough answers that would allow their burning and churning inner artistic drive to find its practical expression. They knew that there had to be a waiting world, hungering for the expressions of joy, loveliness and purity of design that they longed to express in their work.

Meanwhile, Richard, who loved his teaching, at first had not wanted to join the commercial venture. He was, however, supportive and contributed valuable advice. He continued to teach while Victoria created and sold as many pottery pieces as she herself could produce for a New York City store called the Gazebo. The store had been established to provide an outlet for artists and artisans. This meant Victoria and Richard would often work all night and then drive to New York to offer their pottery for sale.

Eventually the inner struggle found breakthroughs. They began creating objects that brought out the child in everyone. Their work became play. Fresh, often wild, ideas fairly flew into being. Their motivation became what is today the mission statement for the entire company: *"To bring homeward complements home, to reveal freedom, jubilance and purity."*

They gained further encouragement from open-minded, joy-seeking art lovers who began collecting the work. It was evident that the fanciful, fresh ideas were showing promise of becoming more and more tangible, that something very big was going on.

Recognizing that Victoria needed him, Richard took a leave of absence from his teaching (actually never to return), and in 1983 he joined Victoria on a full-time basis in behalf of MacKenzie-Childs, Ltd.

Finally a special breakthrough day arrived. An executive with Neiman-Marcus was attracted to Victoria and Richard's booth at a home furnishings show. He was captivated by their merchandise and arranged for a review of the couple's artistic endeavors at the Neiman-Marcus Texas headquarters. The resultant order (which became on-going) launched MacKenzie-Childs on their road to success.

Asked about their relationship, the couple indicate that it is based on love, true friendship and respect for each other's individuality and ability. They function as co-CEOs. When disagreements occur, they're easily and quickly settled, or the issue is temporarily put in abeyance.

The company's products now include hand-formed capricious pottery, furniture, lamps, tassels and trims, linens, cushions, floor mats, paper products, glassware, enamelware and even elegant trailer interiors.

Victoria and Richard's relationship with their staff, which now numbers 400, is an outstanding example of enlightened management. Both are absolutely devoted to the idea that no one in the organization is to receive any special treatment as a result of his or her position in the company. This goes all the way to the top. Victoria says that neither she nor Richard are to be treated differently than anyone else in the organization. The MacKenzie-Childs are dedicated to helping staff members fully express themselves and rise to their highest possible levels. When it comes to the staff dealing with each other, the Golden Rule is the only rule at MacKenzie-Childs, Ltd.

Victoria and Richard don't have a clearly defined list of duties that they divide. Probably because creativity is such a vital factor in their work, they both jump full-force into their world of concepts and ideas. While the couple doesn't want to limit themselves by five-year plans, they do function with ongoing six-month income and expense projections.

The MacKenzie-Childs's studio is located at Aurora, New York, on what was a dairy farm. Growth has necessitated a continuing expansion of these facilities, which by the fall of 1999 should reach about 120,000 square feet of space.

In 1993 the couple opened their American flagship retail store at 824 Madison Avenue in New York City, currently occupying 6,000 square feet. Soon they will be moving to the Chase-Manhattan Bank Building, where they will have 20,000 square feet.

When customers walk into the New York store, they are greeted by a doorman plus a menagerie of chickens, lizards, singing birds, frogs, fish and Linda the cat. This store also has a delightful tea room. The couple will soon open a new beautiful retail store on Rodeo Drive in Beverly Hills.

Where will it all stop? It's not likely that it ever will. Victoria and Richard MacKenzie-Childs have learned that ideas never need to run out—and we know they won't.

By the way, daughter Heather, who was the prime motivation for her parents' move toward marketing their artwork, is married and living in Paris. Both she and her husband, Nils, also work for MacKenzie-Childs, Ltd., which gives every evidence of continuing its amazing success to the delight of untold thousands of playful, art-loving customers.

(www.mackenzie-childs.com)

Doug and Dot Comm and their Dog, Rom™

© J&E Wyman 1999 World Rights Reserved

The Home Office Luncheon Meeting

RADIANT FLOOR HEATING

Hydroheat Systems and Sales

Dan and JoyAnn Maines
Powell, Wyoming

(Transferred unique skills used working for large firm to small business together...former firm encouraged new venture...work around the clock... successfully moved to area with desired lifestyle)

Among the hundreds of thousands of couples in business together are a group of extremely fortunate people. They are the ones who spent years working for companies, usually large ones, where they developed special skills that could be transferred over to their own independent, small businesses, sometimes with the cooperation of the large firm.

Just such a situation occurred for Dan Maines, a radiant heating applications engineer who had worked for two firms near his home in Simi Valley, California. At one point five people were working with Dan on radiant heating design and installations. Dan developed the way to handle this work on the computer, resulting in a reduction in size of the department to one person. He was encouraged by his employer to take over a part of the work on his own, working nights at home. The company turned over to him the names of actual prospective customers.

However, for seven years Dan continued to spend his days at the company, in effect working two jobs. He took the next step, to go out on his own, again with encouragement and support from his former employer.

Dan and his wife JoyAnn, who up to this time had been following a career of her own as an event coordinator in the catering business, then teamed up to operate the new business.

Working out of their home, they launched forth, with Dan doing all of the actual design work. He also supplied materials and directed installations. JoyAnn was responsible for the administrative work, including bookkeeping and invoicing, plus she assisted in various aspects of the installations, where they have found women to be the hardest workers. This division of responsibilities continues today.

When it comes to marketing and advertising their business, word-of-mouth has been their mainstay, plus they use radio to promote their local business in Wyoming and Montana.

When asked for their advice to other couples who might be considering going into business together, both Dan and JoyAnn agree that the couple must be very supportive of each other, respect each other's opinions, and always be ready to compromise their differences. They both feel that each partner should have his and her own offices, thereby allowing each other sufficient room.

After living in California for ten years, the couple decided to move their home and their home-based business to Powell, Wyoming, JoyAnn's home town. Powell's less frantic lifestyle, accompanied by the type of outdoor life the Maines enjoy, has served them well. They've been in Powell for six years and feel that the move was one of the best things they've ever done. Dan admits that one of the advantages of working on his own with JoyAnn in Powell is that he now has more time to go fishing! Once again we find a couple in business together, free to move to an area that can provide a much desired lifestyle.

The Maines and their six-year-old daughter are a happy, productive family, living where they want to live. Their working arrangement allowed them to spend very valuable time with their daughter in the important years before she went off to school.

An oddity that results from Dan's unusual working hours—often through most of the night—is that neighbors who don't know about his schedule and who see him spending lots of time in the yard during the daytime say, "What do you do...where do you work?"

Dan and JoyAnn are now operating their successful, specialized business. Their experience reveals a *modus operandi* that potentially applies to many people who have a unique skill that is transferable from a large company to an independent operation. Their story should inspire others with unique transferable skills.

Doug and Dot Comm and their Dog, Rom™

© J&E Wyman 1999 World Rights Reserved

The In-laws Visit

CATALOG PRODUCERS

(Travel Products)

Magellan's Catalog

John and Gloria McManus
Santa Barbara, California

(Had great idea based on knowledge of field... one gave up previous job, then the other...grew from home-based to three warehouses and 90 employees...mutual understanding, selflessness, camaraderie, dedication and success)

John and Gloria McManus traveled extensively together as PanAm employees. And they kept their eyes and ears open while they traveled. Ultimately, an idea hit them to research and produce a significant, quality catalog of needed and desired travel items.

They began their research by talking to travelers everywhere to determine their preferred travel products. They also compiled a never-ending list of currently available travel items. Quite naturally, their own extensive travel placed them in a unique position to be sensitive to the potential needs of the marketplace.

It took about 18 months from the moment that they hit on the concept until that great day when the couple's first travel catalog actually came off the press.

John was the first to give up his job to focus on their new project, while Gloria stayed on at her position for seven months, maintaining their income flow.

John started out with a Macintosh computer, took some computer classes, and he was ready to work. Together they made their final decisions as to the products to be featured in the catalog.

Next, John proceeded to do all the layout work, wrote the descriptive copy, took the photos with a 35 mm camera, selected the printer and supervised full production.

The McManuses bought a list of known travelers and mail order shoppers from a list broker. This first effort was disappointing, but John and Gloria were undaunted.

John began writing and sending out press releases to suitable publications, and this created the "buzz" needed to get the business going.

At first the couple filled orders out of their home from merchandise that was stacked in their living room and bedroom. Catalogs were everywhere! They worked that way for nearly two years, then in the spring of 1991, they moved into a warehouse in Santa Barbara, by the beach. Readers who are familiar with Santa Barbara, California, will realize that the McManuses, like so many couples in business together, selected a setting that contributes to a very desirable lifestyle.

Today they have further expanded, employing 90 people and occupying three warehouses. Early on they decided to operate with their own staff from their own warehouses rather than farm out most of the needed services. This way they are able to answer customers' product questions directly and provide better service.

Humorous situations have developed, however, such as the time a customer phoned to say she wanted to order a traveler's alarm clock, but wanted to hear a selection of alarm sounds. The service representative lined up all of the alarm clocks and, one by one, turned on each alarm so that the customer could make her selection.

John and Gloria feel that marriages are stronger when couples are in business together, because each partner is required to maintain consistent, clear communication. It's obvious that the McManuses are outstanding examples of this. Their exciting success is living testimony that their philosophy works!

(www.magellans.com)

CATERING

Confident Caterers

Wayne and Shawn Whitescorn
Medford, Oregon

(Positive attitude...great confidence in each other...moved location for affordability... overcame obstacles with ingenuity...instead of working in separate restaurants became successful caterers together)

Picture a very able young chef and an efficient, outgoing waitress, both working at an Italian restaurant in Santa Cruz, California.

If you're thinking that they met and fell in love, married and are now operating a successful catering business about 400 miles further north in Medford, Oregon, you're right on target!

Those are the outside edges of the happy story we're about to detail for you. It's the story of Wayne and Shawn Whitescorn, two very likable, personable, hard-working, creative young people, who didn't want to work separately. They're in Medford because they followed the advice of friends who had also moved there from California and found it more affordable.

And it's working! They love what they're doing, plan and talk about their business all the time and overcome adversity by finding unique solutions. They particularly help each other to avoid procrastination, adhering to a policy of *do it now!*

Returning to their beginnings for a moment, Wayne, who didn't attend a culinary school, had a natural talent for cooking and a great desire to learn everything about it. He constantly researched and talked to other chefs. He has a gift for seasoning and for putting certain foods together—truly a natural!

Shawn started her career in Santa Cruz at the very first step on the ladder, bussing tables. From there she became a fine waitress, and eventually was promoted into restaurant management.

After moving to Medford, the couple divided up into two different restaurant jobs, working different hours—and they didn't like it. What to do? They reasoned that the $5,000 they'd very laboriously saved for a down payment on a house could be better used toward the business they hoped to have together. They bought a computer, a printer, some supplies, had a logo designed and made the huge jump into their own catering business.

Not being able to afford to start with their own kitchen, they rented daytime kitchen time at the dinner restaurant where Wayne first worked when they arrived in Medford. They went to garage and swap sales to pick out various items that they needed for their new business.

After three years they felt growing pains. They were too busy for the present kitchen rental arrangement and moved their operation to warehouse space that was built to their specifications—just in time to service the largest catering job they'd had up to that point! And their growth has continued.

Is everything always rosy in their relationship? Pretty much! Of course they have disagreements, which they settle quickly. They consider each other's point of view, resolve the difference and move forward.

Eventually Wayne and Shawn purchased their own home in the area. They have exchanged the beach life of Santa Cruz for the lakes and rivers of Medford, still enjoying the outdoor lifestyle.

The Whitescorns have a very affirmative attitude toward their employees. They never forget that they, too, were employees, and they remember and consider the challenges they faced. They try their best not to let situations develop where employees might feel resentment.

As far as their customers are concerned, they've learned that by being flexible and adapting to changing requirements, they just might be pushed into a new positive direction that could help their business.

That's the story of the Whitescorns of Medford, Oregon—truly a bright spot in the world of couples in business together!

Doug and Dot Comm and their Dog, Rom™

© J&E Wyman 1999 World Rights Reserved

To My Valentine

Furniture Stores

Country Farm

John and Mary (Koko) Harris
Newcastle, Maine (2) Bath, Maine (1)

(Twenty-six years in business...on farmlike Maine property...three successful stores...major decisions shared...many on staff there over 20 years...try not to let the business take over lives... children grew up with the business...both hold private pilot's licenses)

The state of Maine offered John and Koko Harris the lifestyle they wanted. Starting their business in 1972, they ultimately established and still operate three successful furniture stores.

In addition to their business accomplishments, they raised three children, educating them in their community's fine school system. They purchased shares in a schooner, which provided travel and work opportunities for the family. Both John and Koko learned to fly and obtained their private pilot's licenses.

To go back to their earlier days, they both attended college in Vermont. Koko then taught elementary school for two years, while John served in the U. S. Navy as a supply officer. Ultimately he worked for the Navy Department in Washington, DC.

Eventually they began a search for an affordable business opportunity in Maine. They saw an ad for a home and business on a farmlike property, which seemed like a dream to them. The business that came with the house was a furniture store located in an authentic barn, which made for an outstanding, country setting.

The couple closed the deal with the former owner, and John and Koko took over the existing inventory on a consignment basis—and they were in business! Their expansion into two additional Maine communities testifies to their success.

With the store on their property, their children grew up close to the business, though John and Koko have tried not to let the business take over their lives. Like others in this book, the Harrises made it a rule not to take business to bed. Of course, the business was tremendously demanding at the start when it was not uncommon for one or more of the family to work 72-hour weeks.

At first Koko devoted herself to sales work, allowing her to spend time with their youngest child. Later she added advertising to her responsibilities. John, who has been blessed with a diplomatic manner, handles problems that might come up with customers. Both John and Koko share in the decision-making process, though Koko, with a smile, admits that John has been known to make decisions without checking with her. She adds however, that his unilateral decisions usually turn out to be all right.

John now works at their Newcastle store, where Koko spends two days a week. She is also at their store in Bath for two days, and spends one day in their showroom, Country Farm Furniture, The Day House. Once each year, the two of them travel to North Carolina to attend furniture shows.

Their Country Farm stores have very low staff turnover. Some have been with them for over 20 years. Today a daughter-in-law manages one of the stores.

A humorous side to the Harris's story occurred when three lambs had been abandoned by their mothers and the Harris's son was caring for them, bottle-feeding them in the kitchen. A seven-year-old cousin came to visit and returned home and told his teacher that his cousins had "sheep in the kitchen and furniture in the barn!" The teacher didn't believe him, so the cousin said, "You can call my mom!" The teacher called and learned that it was indeed true, since the barn was a furniture store and the kitchen scene was an effort to save the abandoned lambs.

The story of John and Koko Harris is an outstanding success story, involving family, business and exciting outside activities!

Doug and Dot Comm and their Dog, Rom™

© J&E Wyman 1999 World Rights Reserved

No Competition Here

Mattress Factory

Coachella Valley Mattress Company

Ted and Linda Barnett
Indio, California

(From social emphasis to "business first"... learned the new business prior to taking over... worked doubly hard and long in early years... upgraded equipment and methods...paid back loan...emphasize humor)

The Barnetts have been married 18 years and in business together for the past 11.

Ted had been in construction and Linda was a waitress. They were a couple who loved their active social life. However, events found Linda without a job, and Ted thinking more and more about building something for their future years.

They spotted an ad for what they called a "mom and pop" factory for sale in Indio, California, near Palm Springs. It was a small mattress factory that they considered a "diamond in the rough."

So Ted and Linda made the big decision to go into business together, purchase the factory and change their lifestyle. And change they did! They understood their new commitment and were willing to do whatever was necessary to make it work.

First of all they made a deal with the former owners for Linda to spend the entire month that the deal was in escrow working gratis to learn everything possible about the business. The Barnetts also contacted other mattress companies and suppliers, intensively researching all aspects of the new business.

As for initial financing, the couple put up a sizable down payment from their own funds, and the previous owner carried the paper for the balance—a loan the Barnetts paid back in eight years!

Ted and Linda discovered that the previous owners had been putting in 30-hour weeks. The Barnetts figured that by working very hard and putting in much more time, they should be able to build the business. Driven by a fear of failure, each of them actually worked some 50 to 80 hours a week! Goodbye social life!

Ted and Linda not only learned the business, but upgraded equipment and methods. They made mattresses all day and made deliveries all night! Their initial factory encompassed 4,000 square feet. Their new factory is in a 23,000-square-foot building that includes a 5,000-square-foot showroom, the largest in their desert area. The mattresses are assembled in the back. They now have three additional employees.

After learning the business, the Barnetts focused on marketing—using television, yellow page advertising and public relations.

Their biggest challenge came some years down the road, after they sold their business to another party, who then sued the Barnetts. After a trying year of legal problems, during which time Ted and Linda truly stuck together, the business was awarded back to them. That was five years ago, and they've been running it successfully ever since.

Today they laugh when they think of what they went through over this difficult period. In fact they think laughing and an ever-present sense of humor are vital to success. Ted says "If you can learn to manage humor and inject it when things tend to be getting out of hand, it can benefit all concerned."

The Barnetts laugh about a situation where a very large gentleman (a friend) sat on a couch in their showroom, and broke it. Since then they've tried to avoid having exceptionally large customers lie down on mattresses to test them.

On the same subject, Linda, admitting that although she's willing to work hard and long, says, "Owning your own business is a lot more work and often more stressful than working for somebody else. By being ready to laugh at the situations that develop, 'cartoonizing them,' you can keep a healthy perspective, and things comes out all right."

CONSTRUCTION

Kylander Construction

Rick and Marcia Martin
Powell, Wyoming

(Moved here seeking solid small-town values... bought a going business...retained former name—no ego problem...learned and expanded... management style with crews is to work hard, have fun)

A long-established, specialized construction company in Powell, Wyoming, with a fine reputation was for sale.

The owner ran a blind ad seeking a buyer. The company dealt with gravel and asphalt, paving parking lots, driveways and town roads in the Bighorn Basin of Wyoming.

At that time, Rick and Marcia Martin were living in Southern California. Marcia, a native Californian, was the office manager of a specialty company and Rick, who was born and reared in Powell—a far cry from his Southern California lifestyle—was in corporate management for a large oil firm.

Asked how they met, Rick answers while Marcia giggles. "Through a computer dating service—doesn't everyone in California?"

After meeting, dating and marrying, the Martins both realized that Southern California had become too crowded for them. Rick was eager to relocate back to his native Rocky Mountain area, and Marcia, who had a few qualms about small town living since she had always lived in Los Angeles, was ready to make a move, trusting Rick's judgment.

They checked out the ads in a Billings, Montana, newspaper, and found the blind ad for the construction company, which turned out to be Kylander Construction. What's more, the owner was well known to Rick.

The first thing Rick noticed was the vitality and healthy appearance of Mr. Kylander, who was then in his mid-70s. Rick took this as a very positive sign that here was the kind of business he'd enjoy. Marcia was with him on the decision, and the Martins and Mr. Kylander had a deal.

Rick then went back to Los Angeles and he and Marcia made arrangements to leave their current positions. His company was offering an early retirement plan—so he took it.

Next came the management essentials for the new endeavor, especially financing. Rick knew that in Powell, you can look someone in the eye, come up with a reasonable business proposition, and go do it on a solid foundation of mutual trust. He prepared a 50-page business plan and presented it to a small, local bank. The fact that Rick had gone to school with the banker assured him a fair audience.

Marcia became the firm's president, taking over all administrative duties, while Rick spent the first year working with the crews, learning what asphalt looked like when it was in place—true on-the-job training. Not surprisingly, the company didn't grow much during its first year in the Martins' hands.

Marcia became comfortable running the office, but her challenge was understanding the language of the new venture. One of their smartest moves was to retain the name, Kylander, since it was well known and had a sterling reputation. Fortunately, they had no ego problems to stand in their way.

Marcia, as a result of her natural friendliness and good spirit, easily made friends in her new community and quickly felt at home. In addition to her work, she enrolled at the local community college, taking courses in business management.

Now she is taking correspondence courses toward her bachelor's degree from the University of Wyoming. She is also very active in the local Chamber of Commerce and will be serving on its board of directors.

Rick has a refreshing management style. Each day he tells his crews, "Work hard, have fun!" You can be sure they welcome this approach.

After learning the business, the Martins entered into a growth phase, and purchased a large mobile asphalt plant and a portable crusher. This enabled them to handle jobs as far away as 100 miles from their base. It's interesting to note that asphalt is made up of about 93 percent crushed rock. The rest is hot oil.

Quite naturally their paving operation shuts down from November to April, due to inclement weather. They reduce their staff of 20 to the number of people they need for their continuing work, selling crushed gravel.

Asked how they function as a couple in business together, the Martins state that they make all important decisions together. They have also agreed that Rick will stay out of Marcia's office work and Marcia won't enter into Rick's world of job estimates and crew schedules. The couple thoroughly enjoy their life and their business together and get along fine.

Occasionally Marcia likes to drive the 90 miles to Billings to go out for dinner and a show. They've done this six times in about six years. It's obvious that Rick doesn't exactly like to travel.

The Martins' move from Southern California to the small town of Powell, Wyoming, has worked out beyond their expectations. Their achievements in their growing business and their adjustment to a change in lifestyle are to be greatly admired.

Doug and Dot Comm and their Dog, Rom™

© J&E Wyman 1999 World Rights Reserved

Planning the Vacation

Limousines—Transportation Services

At Your Service

Mike and Alison Chandler
Carmel, California

(Planners and goal setters...meaningful mission statement...enlightened, broad view of their business...high standard of excellence...definite division of duties... best friends)

In Carmel Valley, California (offering a great lifestyle of itself), you'll find Mike and Alison Chandler at the controls of a busy—in fact teeming—transportation business.

Married for five years and in business for three, the Chandlers (with their seven cats and two dogs) are building their business with a definite goal in mind. Their timetable is set so that eventually they can afford more help to free Alison sufficiently to raise a family while managing their business from home.

And be assured that business is good. From their first day in business, the Chandlers earned a profit. Their second year they doubled the first year's volume. And the third year, they doubled the second's.

Visiting with the Chandlers, one is immediately impressed with their professionalism and know-how, an aura that belies their actual ages, which is thirtyish. Far from taking the myopic view, the Chandlers vigorously announce they're not in the limo business, they're in the transportation business. They'll take customers virtually anywhere they want to go in their choice of vehicle. Their fleet consists of two Rolls Royces, one 1951 Bentley, plus Lincoln Town Cars, vans and stretch limousines.

Prior to operating this business, Alison Chandler was teaching school while Mike was working for a hotel, arranging guest transportation. He learned of an existing limousine service for sale. The couple bought it. They immediately set to work out what began as a sensitive area—division of duties. And they did it successfully.

Basically, Alison took over bookkeeping and administrative activities, while Mike accepted responsibility for contacting hotels and, what he calls, "the heavy stuff," arranging for insurance and purchasing the vehicles. They divided up supervision in such areas as the immaculate condition of vehicles, chauffeur training, maintenance, etc.

While the Chandlers obviously love to work together, they admit that they don't always agree on everything. When this happens, they quickly work out their differences through compromise, determined to never let a problem get out of hand. They're both ready to laugh and admit that their sense of humor certainly helps.

Speaking of humor, strange things happen all the time in this business. For example, a head of state from a Middle Eastern country hired them to drive him to San Francisco International Airport (about an hour-and-a-half away) to return to his country. After the customer got out at the airport and the driver left, the customer discovered that he had left his wallet in the back seat of the car. The wallet contained $20,000 cash!

This episode ended with Mike getting up at midnight and driving back to the airport, catching up with the gentleman, and personally delivering the wallet before his plane left for home.

It's indeed refreshing to visit with a young couple with such a professional approach to their business. The Chandlers work hard. They say that for now, vacations are out of the question, as they take total responsibility for keeping their standards very high. In time the rewards will come. Meanwhile, they are excited about doing everything they can to build a business that offers outstanding service and earns them a proper profit.

Doug and Dot Comm and their Dog, Rom™

© J&E Wyman 1999 World Rights Reserved

His Private Office

Computer Systems, Sales and Support

Organized Information, Inc.

Jim and Bonita Roberts
Scottsdale, Arizona

(Their business is their life...many customers have become best friends...keep an affirmative attitude...all-out effort to succeed balanced by careful profit considerations...react to change... great customer retention)

Every business person who is involved in some way with computers (and who isn't?) knows that advances in technology keep an avalanche of changes constantly hitting their businesses, their software and their systems.

Here's the story of a couple whose actual business is serving the firms who use computers, most of whom need help in keeping up with the changes. It's an everlasting learning and serving experience!

Their story goes back 14 years, when Jim and Bonita were dating. Jim, a math major in college, went into computer programming, and eventually launched his own computer sales and systems business.

They married, and it became a foregone conclusion that Bonita would join Jim in his computer company. The first order of business however, was to get Bonita computer-literate.

Bonita, having worked in the beauty salon business, had an understanding of that field, so the couple took on a distributorship for a computer software firm that sold to the beauty salon trade in Arizona. This became a great help to her in learning about computers.

When they teamed up, their business plan could best be summed up as *hustle, hustle, hustle!* Soon their business took hold. They realized that they were in a business that was subject to constant change, therefore their goal was to develop and stay in their own little niche, keeping their business small and profitable, able to react quickly to industry trends.

Like most couples in business together, Jim and Bonita have divided up their duties both to their liking and to the best advantage of the business. Bonita handles the administrative side—purchasing, writing up proposals, billing and inside sales—while Jim is responsible for outside sales, training and installations.

Immediately after going into business together, the couple recognized that now they were responsible for their own ultimate retirement funds. As a result they vowed to always operate soundly and live within their means.

A good example of their solid financial planning and prudence involved an investment in real estate. The couple purchased a small office building that housed two tenants, plus space for their own office. When one of the tenants required more space, rather than lose a good tenant, the Roberts gave up some of their own space. Today, Jim maintains a small office for himself in the building, but considers his home office his headquarters.

An affirmative attitude has always been vital to the Roberts. Quite naturally, Bonita tends to be somewhat more concerned about the immediate outlook since she handles financials, while Jim focuses on the big picture, not wanting momentary blips to slow him down. A good combination!

Jim says that he learned early-on to never project momentary concerns to potential customers. He recognizes the enormous importance of maintaining a positive climate in every aspect of their business.

A significant indicator of Jim and Bonita's success is that over the years, as industry advances have brought on new systems, they have maintained an excellent record of customer retention. In fact, many customers have been through three or four generations of new systems.

Not surprisingly, the Roberts love their life and their business; the two obviously go hand-in-hand.

Lobster Fishing

Lewis and Linda Kelsey
South Bristol, Maine

(Carrying on family tradition...have about 500 lobster traps...she goes out in their boat with him at five a.m....great relationship...each have separate outside interests...no thought of retirement)

Before we relate details of the story of Lewis and Linda Kelsey and their rugged, exciting life as lobster fishermen, let's spend a day with them.

Warning: We're going to have to get up early.

How early? How about four a.m. We'll meet Lewis at five and tag along as he heads for the wharf to fire up his 34-foot diesel-powered fiberglass boat. We climb aboard, and Lewis sets off for the local lobster co-op, where he collects bait for the day, mattahan and herring.

Incidentally, Lewis is one of 12 owners of the co-op. In addition to these members, about 40 boats sell their catches to the co-op, who then sells and ships the lobsters to restaurants in Boston and other appropriate areas in New England.

Now we head back to the Kelsey's home to pick up Linda who, upon our arrival realizes that her time has arrived to get up and pack a lunch.

Then the adventure really begins. We shove off to sea expecting a good catch of the fabulous tasting Maine lobster. We struggle to get our sea legs, but the effort is worth it as we observe the breathtakingly beautiful Maine coastline.

We watch as Lewis and Linda service about 150 of their 500 traps, which are marked by the Kelsey's own colored buoys. Linda cuts up the bait and puts it into nine-by-five-inch mesh drawstring bags. She ties the drawstrings and fastens them to a line. As Lewis hauls a trap onto the boat, she exchanges the old bag of bait with the fresh one.

Next the lobsters are checked for size. The Kelseys observe the Maine regulations that require throwing back small lobsters, as well as those that are over five inches from the eye socket to the end of the body. These large ones are considered breeding lobsters and are tossed back to assure the future of the industry.

It's interesting to watch as Lewis puts the rest of the lobsters into a wire basket while Linda places rubber bands on the claws to prevent them from biting each other. Then into the tank they go.

Once back ashore at about two in the afternoon, we think our day is over. Not true. Now Lewis must work on the traps and buoys. Finally at about five p.m., he arrives back home, making a 12-hour day.

A normal day for him; a very vigorous, rewarding adventure for us.

Now, for more about the Kelseys.

Lewis and Linda have been married for 32 years. They actually dated in high school and were married when she was 19.

When their children were in school, Linda worked as a teacher's aide, which she loved as she had the same hours at school as the children. For about two years she did painting and wallpapering and also worked at a furniture store.

From the time he was 18, Lewis fished with his dad, keeping alive the family tradition. After his dad passed away, Lewis and Linda became the team they are today. Though he tried to discourage Linda from joining him in his rugged work, she would have no part of that and insisted. At first, when the water became rough, she struggled with seasickness, but with the help of motion sickness pills, she overcame it.

For some time the Kelsey's son and their nephew each went out on the boat with Lewis two days a week, while Linda took over for the other two or three days. Now, it's just Lewis and Linda. Their son lives in Nantucket, has ten traps, and does some lobstering for his enjoyment. Interestingly, when their son comes home for a visit, he enjoys a Maine lobster dinner, as he considers his catches off of Nantucket to be not quite as good.

As one can imagine, Lewis and Linda get along famously—they'd have to, working so closely on their boat.

Separate from their lobstering business, the couple have other interests. His is coin collecting, while Linda is involved with volunteer work that takes her to Vermont three times a year for board meetings. Together they collect pressed glass.

Linda has an idea about which she is very enthusiastic. In connection with their lobstering business, she'd like to develop a bed & breakfast inn geared to those who would like to experience a day in the life of a lobster fisherman. For now, Lewis is a bit reserved about the idea. Time will tell—Linda is pretty persuasive!

Linda began thinking about this idea when she met a young lady who was working on a research project on Maine businesses that were over 100 years old. Linda mentioned that Lewis's father and grandfather had both fished before him. This interested the researcher, so Linda invited her and her mother to stay with them overnight, get up early and follow Lewis through his day, photographing everything that interested her. The researcher took hundreds of pictures, which were ultimately displayed at the Augusta State Museum, the University of Maine, and there is also one of Lewis in the Governor's office.

As for retirement, Lewis says, "When you die, you quit." It's obvious that the family tradition will be around for a long, long time.

The Kelseys live a rich, full life. We hope Linda's bed & breakfast idea becomes a reality. Then many people would be able to also enjoy the day we hypothetically shared with this outstanding couple, happily married…in business.

Doug and Dot Comm and their Dog, Rom™

© J&E Wyman 1999 World Rights Reserved

Duties Divided by Proclivities

Sporting Goods/ Clothing Store

War Surplus Store

Tim and LeAnne Kindred

Powell, Wyoming

(Two surprising stores in one...bought and learned the business...his past retail experience helped...she computerized it...they added an in-depth archery department...ready to see the humorous side)

In 1989 Tim and LeAnne Kindred met on a softball team's trip in Denver, Colorado. This turned out to be a very significant meeting. It wasn't long before they were married.

As for their business backgrounds, LeAnne had been gaining valuable experience in bookkeeping and computers, while Tim, as a result of various jobs, was acquiring a solid background in retail.

They didn't want to live in a big city, but desired an area that they felt would be conducive to raising a family and, at the same time, they hoped to own a business together. LeAnne's mother and father had operated a business, so that concept was very natural for her.

While the couple was working in Denver, LeAnne's family heard of a job in Powell, LeAnne's home town, that appeared to be right for Tim. It was. They both agreed that Powell would be the place, and off they went. Tim started his new job and at the same time began to think about a business to purchase.

Tim was aware of the War Surplus Store, which had been in business for some 25 years. In fact he felt that someday he'd like to buy it. Meanwhile, a friend of LeAnne's happened to be talking to the owner of the store, and told her about the Kindreds.

One day the couple was having lunch at a sandwich shop directly across from the store when they saw a woman heading across the street in their direction. This woman was the owner of the War Surplus Store. She approached the couple and asked them to come to the store and talk to her. She then said that the store was for sale, and that she'd like to sell it to someone who would appreciate it and do right by it. The end result was that Tim and LeAnne became the new owners of the War Surplus Store!

The couple easily arranged financing at the local bank since the business had such a fine track record.

That was about three years ago. Life became pretty wild for Tim and LeAnne. They purchased and moved into their new home in September, had their second baby in October and took over the store in January. It's been relatively calm ever since.

Once the store was theirs, the Kindreds did a little remodeling, transforming an unused area into display space, and learned the business. LeAnne computerized the store's systems, including inventory control.

The women's department offers a wide variety of well-known brands. The Kindreds have added children's clothes. The clothing section also features men's work wear, including full lines of work and hunting boots.

The sporting goods department carries everything from complete camping, hunting and fishing equipment, to a newly developed, in-depth archery department that Tim has made into a growing operation. Along with selling bows, arrows and special features for the true archery buff, Tim gives advice to the many newcomers to the sport.

Women too have begun to take up archery. They take part in competitions where three-dimensional animal targets are used. When actually hunting, women archers, just as the men, are apt to perch in a tree waiting for their prey.

Not surprisingly, in their second year the couple's archery business doubled its first year's volume.

Tim and LeAnne employ four people. They have been fortunate in having good people who stay with them.

The couple's two small children will, when they are old enough, undoubtedly become very aware of their parents' business, probably spending good learning time at the store. Meanwhile, Tim and LeAnne consider themselves very fortunate in having fine one-on-one childcare in place during these pre-school years.

The couple divide their time and duties according to their natural talents and experience. LeAnne's bookkeeping background obviously makes her a natural to everything related to administrative work. She puts in about 80 percent of her time in that area, spending the balance working on the sales floor.

Tim is heavily involved with buying duties as well as waiting on the trade. As previously indicated, the enlarged, very successful archery department takes up a good deal of his time.

Tim and LeAnne have a great sense of humor. Each is company president on alternate months. Tim is a hero, claiming December, while poor LeAnne has January.

The War Surplus Store (really two stores in one) offers pleasant surprises to walk-in traffic. Tim and LeAnne's special touch has continued the former owner's tradition and has added elements that have already helped move the business forward. We wouldn't be surprised if the best is yet to come!

Doug and Dot Comm and their Dog, Rom™

© J&E Wyman 1999 World Rights Reserved

The Salary Cut

ARCHITECTS

(Plus several other entrepreneurial ventures)

Garcia Architects, Inc.

Gil and Marti Correa-Garcia
Santa Barbara, California

(A classic case...individually each did well, together they boomed...she mastered her early duties and helped move them into new entrepreneurial areas...he added city council membership...architecture still vital)

Here is a situation whereby it can be said that ***one plus one equals*** at least ***four!*** And that's not an exaggeration.

When Santa Barbara architect Gil Garcia married Marti Correa in 1983, it was agreed that Marti would join Gil's business to help manage the office—generally with bookkeeping.

Marti who had been doing office work in the Los Angeles area, not only mastered what was expected of her, but greatly expanded her horizons. And that meant that the team of Gil and Marti were headed for exciting growth

For a moment, let's go back to earlier years. As a young man, Gil Garcia, desperately wanted to be an architect. He wanted it bad enough to take the *self-taught* route. And that meant eight long years of supervised apprenticeship, plus design courses at night.

A long pull, but he made it. In 1973 Gil became a licensed architect. He was good and his clients knew it. Riding the crest of one of California's vigorous real estate booms, Gil had the opportunity to show what he could do.

In addition to architectural assignments for clients, he entered into the commercial and residential real estate development and management business.

Then came Gil's marriage to Marti. Branching out beyond bookkeeping and clerical duties, one of her areas became the management of the commercial and residential properties.

Of course, the Garcias' basic architectural business continued to be their prime activity. And they worked together exceptionally well. Each had their own areas of expertise. Marti says, "That's right, Gil makes the money and I spend it!"

Humor is very evident in their hardworking world. They tell of the time that a client became very concerned about the plans for her kitchen. At this point, Gil quickly said, "Marti is a kitchen expert!" Marti thought, "What is he saying?" (Marti had just taken a very major roll in the design of the Garcias' own kitchen, giving him all the advice in the world—and now she was going to pay for it!) The client began to ask Marti specific kitchen-type questions. Marti quickly became an expert on counter-tops, stoves, refrigerators and other kitchen appliances. The potentially sticky moment became satisfactorily unstuck. Marti later commented to Gil, "I'm glad I'm an expert on something!"

Eventually the Garcias' architectural business (now statewide) grew so that the company owned two airplanes with corporate pilots. When the economy returned to normal and as other activities began to take hold, Gil and Marti reduced the size of their architectural staff and sold the airplanes.

Fourteen years ago, an opportunity to make application to construct, own and operate a new UHF television station in Santa Barbara came to the couple's attention. Gil felt that Marti would be a natural to head up this venture. He encouraged her to organize a partnership with two other minority women as general partners. He became a limited partner, to invest in the project but not be involved with direct management.

At the time we talked to the Garcias, they had just returned from Washington, DC, where Marti appeared before the appropriate government officials in connection with their application. Gil knows that Marti is more than equal to this exciting opportunity, which has already required 14 years of patience.

During the Garcias' exciting adventures, another business opportunity came along—something else that Marti could successfully handle—a tire shredding business. It had been decided that a land-fill in the Los Angeles area contained too many tires. Marti started the tire-shredding business, successfully handled the situation, and eventually sold the business to a former partner of Gil's.

As time moved along, Gil found himself becoming more and more involved in community activities. Marti also turned some of her attention to doing volunteer work for worthwhile non-profit causes. Gil ultimately was elected to the Santa Barbara City Council, where he serves with distinction. He is devoted to working for the good of future generations.

The Garcias have made it a point to often have exchange students stay at their home. It's not unusual for Marti to dash home to cook a great meal for these students, whom the couple refer to as their extended family.

As for advice for other couples who are contemplating going into business together, they both agree that you must be the very best of friends. In addition, they recommend that each give the other enough space to grow. It's obvious that Gil has greatly encouraged Marti's growth into new areas in which she has greatly succeeded.

While they try not to bring business home with them, they laughingly admit that it can't be done. There are days when they can't talk to each other all day. Following one of those days, just as they were about to drop off to sleep, Marti said, "Gil, wake up, I need some quality time to talk to you!" Understandable.

What a wonderful example of a couple being stronger together than they would be if each were on their own. The Garcias are to be congratulated.

Business Education

Southwestern School of Real Estate

Burt and Susan Sweetow

Scottsdale, Arizona

(Vision for new learning concept...extension of past experience...able to adjust to change... perfect matches for differing duties...versatile teaching capabilities...ever-present humor... resiliency...student loyalty)

When you meet with Burt and Susan Sweetow, be ready to be stimulated by ideas, to shift into meaningful subjects of current concern, and most of all, be ready to laugh. A lot!

From this you can rightfully gather that the Sweetows are an alert, very knowledgeable couple with a wide variety of interests, not the least of which is their real estate school. And yes, like most of the couples in this book, they admit to being best friends as well as husband and wife and partners in their business.

Burt and Susan were married in South Bend, Indiana in 1957, where Susan began her real estate career. She continued in real estate after the couple moved to Scottsdale in 1976, when her husband joined her in the business.

Burt, who was experienced in management and excellent at following through on legal and administrative matters, took over those areas. Susan was outstanding at selling and meeting with the public. Their division of duties is an example of partners with totally different talents being perfectly matched to differing areas of their business.

It was while Burt and Susan were taking their required courses in continued real estate education that they realized there could be another approach to real estate teaching and learning. While they felt that a good job was being done by the existing schools, the Sweetows thought that more informal, in-depth student participation in discussions could offer a viable, fresh approach that would be very helpful to the students.

They researched the idea among knowledgeable and authoritative people in the industry. They studied, planned and planned and planned some more. Next they learned and met the requirements of the state Department of Real Estate. Eventually, goals clearly in mind, they were ready to launch their new endeavor.

True to their fresh concept, the couple and their instructors made a point of teaching in a relaxed, informal atmosphere. The students sat comfortably around a large conference table in a setting that encouraged questions and interactive discussions. The Sweetows, incidentally, became very adept at filling in when a scheduled instructor couldn't be present.

Early on an interesting by-play between the couple came about at an extremely rare time when only one or two students showed up for a class. They had previously established a policy that if this ever happened, they would still teach the class, as they felt they owed it to the students. However, when this occurred, Burt would disparagingly say, "Oh, only two people showed up!" To which Susan would reply, "Hooray! Two people know about us and have come to our class!"

That's a classic example of the glass being either half empty or half full! In actuality, the couple presents a fine balance because of their tendency to look at things a bit differently—and they do harmonize in their ultimate mutual decisions.

Humor is an important factor in the world of the Sweetows. They love to tell of the time that a student raised a question unrelated to anything they'd been talking about: "Whatever happened to maple furniture?" Trying to hide her laughter, Susan intentionally dropped an eraser on the floor in order to bend down and hide. Two other students who had caught her eye also began quietly laughing. Ultimately all three began to shake with laughter to the point that Susan couldn't pick up the eraser or stand up for what seemed like an eon.

Surely, like all couples in business, the Sweetows have faced challenging moments. At these times they have shown great resiliency and an ability to analyze the situation and adjust to change. When necessary they have reduced expenses, but always in areas that do not affect the quality of the teaching.

Burt and Susan Sweetow are accomplishing their goals. Over the years their school has established an outstanding record of students returning for their continuing education. It's no wonder—because they give so much of themselves to everything they do.

Doug and Dot Comm and their Dog, Rom™

© J&E Wyman 1999 World Rights Reserved

Hiring

DESIGN-WALLPAPER

Wallpaper Plus

Lee and Fola Miller
Palm Desert, California

(Marriage and a new business in their 50s...she had been a designer and he, in real estate... combined past talents into new mix...found a niche with retail application...true mutual respect)

Lee and Fola Miller can stand tall as representatives of the group of dynamic entrepreneurs who were already in their 50s when they found each other—and then founded a business together.

They were also smart enough to analyze their past experience, talents and present desires, and mold them into a suitable retail application that has become their very own niche.

Fola was an interior designer for 20 years. Lee was a real estate broker and was ready for a change. Initially they teamed up in connection with Fola's residential design work. She handled substantial design jobs, and he, with his contractor's license, contracted the work. At first they enjoyed this and all went well. After about two years, due to difficult large clients, they sought a change.

Offering design services by way of their own retail store, selling related products then occurred to them. Lee had a degree in business plus the past experience of owning a business, while Fola had a broad spectrum of significant design experience. This meant to Lee that Fola should basically be the key person in the operation.

They knew that a natural division of duties would come about without stepping on each other's toes. And that's what happened. It was evident that Fola wasn't mechanically inclined, so that phase fell to Lee. He took on the bookkeeping, drafting and construction phases of their work.

They ultimately found a wallpaper store for sale and bought it at a fair price. When their first lease was up, they found a new location that better served their needs, and made the big move.

In developing their business, the Millers knew they couldn't compete price-wise with the large stores. At the same time they knew they were attracting a clientele that was somewhat older and in a higher economic group—very often second home owners.

Putting these two marketing facts together, they determined to stay with a better, higher quality product rather than scratch around for the lowest priced merchandise.

All-in-all, it took about six years to clearly establish their business, built around their desired niche. The past two years have brought a successful realization of their goals for Fola's design work as well as for their retail products.

On the personal side, Lee and Fola have the advantage of learning from their past marriages and business experiences. They have a better perspective and know when to back off from a difference of opinion with grace, sometimes agreeing to disagree. They know the importance of letting the other party grow. They endeavor not to take their business home with them, but do grow a bit wistful when speaking of vacations. So far, only the week before Christmas has been available; they hope that some day that will change.

The Millers have a ready sense of humor, recounting the time Fola was with a customer whose furniture was being delivered on a hot August day. The husband drove up, gave his wife a hug and a kiss and a piece of paper. She read it, batted her eyes at him, and said, "I'm not overdrawn, you're under- deposited."

Lee tells of the time he was installing a pop-up television set and was sprawled out with his head under the cabinet. The client came in and asked how he learned to do that. Lee said, "I'm one of those men who was born handy instead of rich." The client replied, "Well, I've been both, and rich is better!"

The Millers are an example of overcoming adversity and then finding a new successful plateau.

Doug and Dot Comm and their Dog, Rom™

© J&E Wyman 1999 World Rights Reserved

Buying the New Car

BED AND BREAKFAST

Sunset House

Dennis and Camille Fike
Carmel, California

(Working together lets them really know and appreciate each other...goal: to provide a haven for guests, contribute to their well-being...days start at five a.m....be able to laugh at yourself... only one week-long vacation in four years... difficult to find employees that meet their standards)

The Fikes have had two distinct business careers that have filled their lives. The second one, on-going right now, finds them totally in business together, and loving it.

Dennis makes it very clear that the only two regrets he has in his life are, one, that he didn't marry Camille sooner (they've been married for 34 years), and two, that they didn't go into their current business sooner!

That paints a pretty good picture of their relationship. There's a lot of warmth, love and respect for each other's talents in evidence here.

For a glance at their first career, we go back to the days when the Fikes lived in the San Francisco Bay Area. Dennis owned a retail carpet store for many years. Camille worked part time at the store until their two boys (now adults) were in junior high school, when she opened her own home-decorating business. They loved to entertain and, living in a spacious home, enjoyed hosting large groups. This love of welcoming people into their home foretold their eventual career together.

As time went on, Dennis felt a growing desire to retire from his retail business and spend more time at home. The couple looked into purchasing income property, but their agent thought that since they were so personable, they should consider going into the bed and breakfast business.

In November, 1991, they sold their home four days after putting it on the market and next, found a very suitable, already existing bed and breakfast in the beautiful town of Carmel-by-the-Sea, California. The home is about two blocks from the ocean. The Fikes are a vivid example of a couple deciding to go into business together and, at the same time, selecting one of America's most picturesque areas in which to work and live.

And they do work hard! The home that they purchased needed a lot of work, which they accomplished as they proceeded in business. Dennis did most of it himself, but both Dennis and Camille enjoyed the labor and, especially, the complete change from their former businesses.

The couple function with a strong mission. Both are religiously oriented, and they endeavor to base their lives on Biblical principles. This gives a strong purpose to their business activity. It is their dream to make their place a haven for all. It has helped them regain their desired focus on life, and they are thoroughly enjoying it. They hope to make a difference in their guests' lives as well.

Sunset House has five rooms that they rent to guests. The Fikes do their own laundry and take delight in maintaining a high standard in everything from towels to daily maintenance to the breakfast trays. Dennis chooses woods for the individual fireplaces, basing his selection on sound, color and scent. He hand splits the logs.

As for their schedule, Dennis begins his day between five and six in the morning. He spends two hours preparing the very special breakfasts. He selects and cuts the fruits, picks the breads and readies everything for Camille to take over. Camille comes in at about seven and fills magnificently crafted food trays with the fruits, breads and jams. They spend the rest of the day doing yard work, maintenance and management.

Their biggest challenge is finding employees who can meet their high standard of service. The result is that in four years, they've only managed one week-long vacation.

Of note is the fact that Dennis and Camille maintain an ever-present sense of humor, feeling that being able to laugh at themselves is vital.

Working together in this, their second career, has made the Fikes appreciate each other more; both say they're better because of the other!

Doug and Dot Comm and their Dog, Rom™

© J&E Wyman 1999 World Rights Reserved

The Joggers

Hardware Store

Powell Valley True Value Hardware

Glen and Nancy Holm
Powell, Wyoming

(Personify solid small-town USA values... properly financed to put on sound footing... separate duties, but back each other up...all-out effort to make it work...rode out negative changes in the economy...now expanded with additional space...best friends)

Glen and Nancy Holm are a couple who personify the solid, down-to-earth values so needed in today's business world. At the same time, their hardware store is very definitely successful. This story shows that knowing one's business, working very hard at it and running it soundly can be a formula for success.

Interestingly, the Holms, like several other couples profiled in this book, chose to operate their business in Powell, Wyoming, where Glen feels a spirit of brotherhood exists.

Married in 1970, Glen and Nancy lived in Laramie and Cody, Wyoming, where for five years they owned a catalog business. Eventually they sold that business and Glen went to work for an oil company.

In 1981 the couple had some ambitious ideas, feeling that owning a substantial business together would give them the opportunity to get ahead. They learned of a desirable building for sale in nearby Powell that they thought would be right for the type of retail operation they had in mind.

They purchased the building, then turned it into a True Value Hardware store. True Value is a well-known hardware co-op. Membership gave the Holms the benefit of volume when it came to purchasing inventory.

Glen and Nancy sold their home and pooled their proceeds with those from the sale of their former business in Cody, then they approached the bank.

The bank responded favorably because they were able to put up 50 percent of the total amount needed for the deal. Best of all, Glen and Nancy were able to go into their new venture adequately financed. It's well known that more businesses fail because they are underfinanced than for virtually any other reason.

The couple opened up their hardware store in 1981. Early-on the oil drilling business was booming, and the employees' paychecks were sizable. Business was good for Glen and Nancy. However, as the cost of importing oil went down, the drilling business in Powell slowed and has never recovered.

Due to the sound manner in which the Holms financed and operated their business (during their early years they put most of their earnings back into the store), they survived the slowdown and have, in fact, expanded. A variety store next door to the Holms' was suffering due to increasing pressure from large retailers. It had not gone out of business, but the end was in sight. This afforded Glen and Nancy the opportunity to buy the business and the building. They were able to close out the inventory and then expand their hardware business.

More evidence of operating soundly is that Glen functions professionally with income and expense projections. Due in good measure to the expansion, these projections call for a very ambitious bottom-line figure, which Glen feels is attainable. He and Nancy are grateful that things have worked out well for them. It's obvious that they made it happen with a lot of dedication and hard work.

Of great significance in the Holms' life is their teenage daughter, of whom they are very proud. She virtually grew up in the store, spending much time there in her early years. She is now a senior in high school.

Glen and Nancy each work at his or her own specialty. Nancy excels with the paperwork, including bookkeeping, which is good since Glen doesn't like that type of work at all. Glen spends much of his time on the sales floor, answering what he calls "the nuts-and-bolts questions," mixing paint, plus handling the rest of the myriad details that come up at a busy hardware store. Nancy, too, finds herself helping out on the sales floor. Over the years they have backed each other up, filling in wherever needed. The Holms have seven employees. The store is open for business seven days a week. In addition to the store, the Holms own some rental property, which adds to their responsibilities. No time for vacations—but that's retail!

Humor plays an important role in the couple's daily business life. They state that it helps to overcome hardships. There have been occasions when a customer might become particularly difficult and almost abusive. At such times, the Holms have spoken up, answering in kind, and the situation evens out. Once Glen had to call a particularly difficult customer an "ornery old coot," at which point he immediately straightened out.

Glen and Nancy are quick to say that they are *best friends*, as is the case with most of the couples profiled in this book.

It seems apparent that the Holms' success, so soundly based, will favorably continue.

Meat Processing

Carlson Meats

Charles and Kristin Carlson
Grove City, Minnesota

(Unique third generation family business, serving a special world of agriculture from a very small town...with full-service meat processing...highest standards...dedicated... successful...happy!)

Here's the story of Chuck and Kristin Carlson's refreshingly different, third-generation, husband and wife-operated, successful business. It's an old-world (but thoroughly modernized) enterprise, employing ten people, located in a very, very small town called Grove City, Minnesota, population 596.

For the Carlson family, it started in 1913 when Chuck's grandfather purchased the business. Grove City, which was originally called Swede Grove, and Carlson Meats, then known as City Meat Market, began their now 86 year relationship. They're still going strong, although the agricultural world they serve has been continually changing. But the Carlsons have adapted.

William Carlson, (known as "Billy Butch") began operations serving the local Scandinavian population, selling fresh cuts of meat, sausages and specialty items. After World War II, William's son, Willard, who had grown up in the business, began working with his dad. Willard changed and expanded the scope of the business in the 1950s and '60s, to include custom processing and frozen meat. In 1955 he had new equipment installed to accommodate the expanded activity.

A significant event took place in 1972. Carlson Meats started USDA inspections, just at the time that federal meat inspection regulations increased. While maintaining these standards has been very expensive, it has certainly been worthwhile, since it has emphasized the high quality that the Carlsons maintain. They are one of the few such meat processing operations in their part of Minnesota to take this step.

Meanwhile, the family saga continues. Willard's young son, Chuck, who also grew up in the business, attended Bethel college, where he was a biology major. Following graduation he secured a summer job at Glacier National Park in Montana driving one of the old red tour buses that are a symbol of the park. Because of their tendencies to jam the gears of the 1930s buses, the drivers are called "jammers." Here Chuck met and fell in love with another summer resort worker, Kristin Olson, who came from a Chicago suburb. Had the couple not met during their summer jobs, they never would have known each other.

Chuck and Kristin were married in 1974 and in 1975, moved back to Grove City and the family business. First the couple became partners in the company and enjoyed working closely with Chuck's dad.

Following Willard's passing in 1983, Chuck and Kristin were fully prepared to take over the operation. They are purchasing the balance of ownership from Chuck's mother, who also works at the shop.

The focus of the business now includes the continuation of the tradition of quality custom meat processing, as well as selling halves and quarters of beef and pork. The retail side of the business also features many varieties of award-winning homemade sausages, some new recipes and some that were used in the early days by grandfather "Billy Butch." Rightfully, Kristin unabashedly announces, "We're good at what we do!"

Chuck and Kristin have three children ages 21, 19 and 15. All have gained valuable work experience at the shop. This summer daughter Katy kept a family tradition alive by working at Glacier National Park. Her dad warned her: "Watch out for the jammers!"

The Carlsons, like so many couples in business together, fell into a very natural division of duties. As Chuck simplifies it, "I do the physical work, and Kristin does the rest." Actually, there's much more to it than that. Chuck is responsible for responding to the farmers who call to have an animal picked up and brought to their plant for processing. After he brings the animal in, Chuck supervises all operations through to cutting into steaks and roasts or whatever cuts of meats were ordered. Chuck also supervises the wrapping, packaging, sausage making and curing. Kristin is responsible for dealing with customers who come to their business, supervises bookkeeping and billing, handles all paper work, and keeps things moving efficiently.

As to their personal relationship as a husband and wife in business, they, like virtually every couple in this book, maintain that a couple in business together must be *best friends*! If they have a difference of opinion, they settle the disagreement as quickly as possible.

It's obvious that Chuck and Kristin are very hard workers. Chuck gets up at 5:25 every morning, and is at the shop by 6. Kristin arrives by 8. During the morning they have very little contact until heading home (six blocks away) for their noon meal. During this break at home, Kristin gets at some of the housekeeping duties (such as starting the washing machine.) Back for the afternoon until at least 4:30; they often find that the work load keeps them at the shop until later.

Both Chuck and Kristin have a ready sense of humor. Kristin starts laughing as she barely begins to relate her number one problem with her husband. Even though she knows he's at the shop, she can never find him when she wants him. He's usually between the equipment, customers, freezers, cubby holes—or who knows where? No matter, she just can't find him when she needs him..

The biggest problem facing the Carlsons is difficulty in hiring qualified help. This appears to be common among couples in business.

So we know the Carlsons work hard. How about their pleasure? Let it be told that Chuck continues a hobby from his boyhood: model railroading. He loves it! Together, they attend railroading shows in Minneapolis and Chicago. At these shows, while Chuck is talking and trading trains, Kristin sells packaged meat at the other end of the table.

The couple also has a cabin in Minnesota, located about a two-hour drive from their home. They go to the cabin on as many weekends as possible. In order to turn their attention away from the meat business, Kristin reads novels to Chuck while they're driving.

And how's this for a nostalgic, romantic event? Ten to 15 times over the past 20 years, Chuck and Kristin have driven the 21 hours to visit Glacier National Park for a two-week vacation. After all, that's where the whole thing started!

On the serious side is the problem of shrinking farms. The couple hope that some day this will turn around, but they can't count on it.

Meanwhile, the Carlsons enjoy their unique business, each other, their children, their hobby and their great life in Grove City, Minnesota!

Doug and Dot Comm and their Dog, Rom™

© J&E Wyman 1999 World Rights Reserved

Canoeing on a Day Off

Restaurant/ Convenience Store

Harborside

Sam and Betsy Graves
South Bristol, Maine

(View restaurant seats 30, plus store...humor prevails...great friendship between them...love their work, location and customers...almost feel like they're retired, entertaining friends—in spite of 70 hour weeks)

Please note in our preview to this story (above) we mentioned that humor prevails. Does it ever!

This is about as hardworking a couple as you're going to find—actually working 70- to 80-hour weeks. How do they do it?

They have a lot of fun!

For example, the Graves, well known and trusted by the town's people, have provided the friendly type of atmosphere where customers comfortably drop off their children while they go about their errands. Not only does the restaurant provide toys for the children, but Sam has a reputation for giving them outlandish advice (all in fun), such as inviting the children to put their feet up on the tables, telling them that it's perfectly all right for them to do that in a restaurant. When their parents return, imagine their horror at the sight that greets them! Sam says, "It's good for the parents—keeps them on their toes!"

Sam, who is criticized by the children for smoking, tells them, "You're right, I shouldn't smoke. The next time you see someone smoking in here, say to them, 'Oh, you big fat stupid—put your feet up on the table and relax!'"

Let's move over to the story of the couple's business. Betsy, who had a retail background, was raised in a family that had their own business, so she was accustomed to all that goes into a family-owned operation.

Sam's family owned a drive-in restaurant, where he worked during his high school years. He spent his adult life prior to his Harborside days in restaurant management.

Married in 1985, three years later both Betsy and Sam were at the point where they wanted a business of their own. Each had been successful working for others, and they felt that the time was right to put the effort in on their own behalf.

After due consideration, the Graves purchased their current building, which is located right at the ocean in the Maine sea coast town of South Bristol. The town, primarily a fishing village, is located about 20 miles from the nearest other small town. Betsy grew up in the area, so this move meant she was coming home.

South Bristol has a year-round population of about 800. In the summer, vacationers, many of whom have second homes, descend to enjoy the beauty and local color. At that time the population doubles.

The building Sam and Betsy purchased contained a convenience store, which they immediately remodeled. They divided up the space to allow restaurant seating for 30 to 40 people. The couple enjoy their situation to the point of feeling that they are basically retired—continually entertaining their wide circle of friends. These friends are the valued customers of the restaurant and store.

Much of this pleasant feeling is created because their place of employment is about ten feet from their home. Incidentally, their home overlooks a wide expanse of the magnificent Atlantic Ocean.

The couple's work schedule shows how their time easily builds up to 70 or 80 hours each week. Betsy does all the baking, while they share the cooking. Betsy starts at seven a.m., when she opens the restaurant, and continues until two in the afternoon, after which she handles the paperwork, goes on errands and makes the desserts for the next day.

Sam comes to work at 11 in the morning. He closes the restaurant at nine, then he does the cleaning.

Regularly, the Graves have two employees, a figure that goes up to six in the summer. Neither Sam nor Betsy have any thoughts of actual retirement, rather their long-range goal deals more with eventually hiring more employees so that they can enjoy more time off. Betsy is involved with community service, serving on the local school board. Both enjoy sports on television. Sam plays tennis and golf, bowls and coaches basketball.

In closing, we are compelled to refer again to Sam and Betsy's ever-ready sense of humor. Once, with 20 customers in the restaurant, Betsy dropped three dozen eggs. Of course she felt like screaming, but instead broke out laughing—a much better solution.

The Graves would advise couples considering going into business together—especially a business that resembles theirs—to be sure that they truly like as well as love each other, because they're going to be together 24 hours a day. Also, not surprisingly, they bring up the need for that ever-ready sense of humor!

Sam and Betsy Graves epitomize a couple who are successful in business, work hard, and truly enjoy their work—as well as each other.

Doug and Dot Comm and their Dog, Rom™

© J&E Wyman 1999 World Rights Reserved

A Growing Business

METAL DETECTORS

Al's Discount Detectors

(Formerly Arizona Al's)

Al and Debbie Jones
Blairsville, Georgia

(From hobby of searching for relics to an established business...set goals...trust each other's abilities...be open-minded...moved location to desired lifestyle)

"Turn your hobby into a full-time business!"

How many times have you heard people say they wish they could do exactly that? Here's the story of a couple who have. What's more, after seven years in business they have moved their home and their business across the country to live their desired lifestyle.

Al Jones, originally from the South but at the time living in Glendale, Arizona, had a very strong hobby—call it a passion—for searching for historical relics. After college Al had various jobs, including working for automotive garages and retail stores. Debbie had been in retail since she was 16. Prior to teaming up with Al on his new project, Debbie was office manager at a public warehouse.

Al started his metal detection equipment business on a part-time basis in 1991, shifting into a full-time business 14 months later. He soon found that in addition to using the metal detection equipment to uncover relics, which had been his great interest, many customers purchase the equipment to search for gold in desert sands or jewelry at beaches.

In 1996 Al and Debbie began working together, partners in their own business. Al desperately needed Debbie's help with bookkeeping and office duties, freeing him for his work with products and, especially, with the customers.

While the hours are long and the effort intense, a plus for the couple is that in this line of work, discovery trips to Europe (searching for relics) are an important part of the couple's overall activity.

The Jones's marketing activities have taken on a new focus with use of the Internet, where they have a Website that Debbie maintains. They also advertise in other appropriate media. The ability to market their products on the Internet has played a major role in allowing Al and Debbie to make their desired move to the Smoky Mountains area.

Debbie says that Al is in charge of coming up with creative ideas, and it's her job to make them a reality. The Jones also cite the importance of remaining open-minded to fresh outside opinions, feeling that stubbornness in this area could block good ideas.

They both agree on the importance of giving each other sufficient space, and they quickly abandon hurt feelings. They allow each other to bring his or her best individual talents to the business.

Al is the planner, believing in goal-setting, and we're sure that their recent move from Arizona to Blairsville, Georgia, is the realization of one of his strongly felt goals.

The couple had long been seeking a slower-paced lifestyle. As we've been pointing out in this book, couples who are in business together are in a wonderful position to combine business and a desired lifestyle, to the advantage of both.

Yes, it is possible to turn a much-loved hobby into a full-time business, providing the product, the know-how, the drive, the work ethic and a ready market that can be efficiently reached are in the mix together. Also, nothing is more important than the individualities of the couple, who must prove that they can work together as a team, find the right division of duties and, incidentally, keep a sense of humor—all points on which Al and Debbie score well.

(www.discountdetectors.com)

Nursery

Roth Gardens

Chris and Tarilee Roth
Draper, Utah

(Grew from two to 100 people...combines his experience, know-how and calming manner with her competence and efficiency...they overcome rough spots quickly... don't bring problems home)

One of our true growth stories, Roth Gardens is a multi-faceted, well-run business located in Utah's Salt Lake Valley. It was founded by Chris Roth nine years ago, and has grown from a staff of the original two to 100 people.

Roth Gardens breaks down into five related divisions: commercial landscape, residential landscape, property maintenance, excavating and the nursery.

At the time that Chris and Tarilee were married almost three years ago, Tarilee was not in the business. In fact she'd held a very fine position with a local firm for five years.

Chris knew the needs of his dynamically growing business and was on the lookout for an additional key person. Several previous experiences with family members had not worked out well for all concerned.

He consulted with his board of directors, and all members of the board felt that his wife Tarilee would be the right one for the job. Chris then asked Tarilee to join him, and she agreed, with one very important qualification. She had him actually sign an agreement that he would be kind to her. Very smart!

They also agreed not to bring problems from the business home at night. They resolved that any business discussion could be held at the office the next day. The result? It's been a year-and-a-half since the couple teamed up, and it's working. It is acknowledged that Tarilee has brought much to the business.

However, it wasn't easy at first. Her duties were to include the purchasing for all five divisions—a major responsibility, particularly since the business was already established as a growing, successful operation. But everything was totally new to Tarilee. At first, she worked in Chris's office, where he became her instructor and support. He was invaluable to her during the learning process. He was patient and kind—in keeping with their signed agreement.

Among Tarilee's challenges was learning both the botanical and common names of the huge number of plants that the nursery orders and sells. At one point, in order to identify the plants she was ordering, Tarilee helped unload the trucks of incoming merchandise, always asking the names of the various plants, their sizes and special features. When she placed her orders, the vendors would provide valuable information to her, which was another significant help.

Specifically, Tarilee's work consists of handling phone calls, and purchasing everything from the merchandise to be sold to the public, to supplies for the office, to tires for their vehicles. Often she'll spend three hours a day endeavoring to get the best possible price for the plants she intends to order.

Tarilee also developed a computer-driven purchase order control system that shifted responsibility from each supervisor over to her computerized purchasing control. This eliminated the former common practice of employees often ordering more than had been approved.

In addition to Tarilee's regular responsibilities, she has learned to operate the Skid-Steer Loader. She's now the loader/

operator in the nursery, moving product and plant for customers. Next she plans to learn to operate the Track Hoe. Tarilee says "Chris may lose all patience while I'm learning that!"

Now, Chris spends about 85 percent of his time in the field, checking on jobs and estimating projects, so he's not present to answer Tarilee's questions. If a major challenge emerges, Tarilee phones or radios him, at which time Chris calms her down with his very positive manner.

Chris has been in the nursery business since his boyhood, but feels that he's still learning. He admits to formerly having a short fuse, but over the years he has acquired a perspective that helps everyone in the company. He's definitely a calming influence.

Chris acts as a counselor to his foremen and helps his employees through problems that affect their performance. His credo is to always make it right for the customer. And he's very firm when it comes to matters of principle and won't tolerate dishonesty or theft.

Currently the business is functioning very smoothly as a result of new, efficient systems that Tarilee has developed. As with any couple in business, there are occasional rough spots, but the Roths always overcome them in short order.

Here is an example of a business that was already a success before the husband and wife teamed up together at the management level. Now it's better with the two of them!

Doug and Dot Comm and their Dog, Rom™

© J&E Wyman 1999 World Rights Reserved

The Romantic Dinner

LINGERIE STORES

Chadwick's of London

Michael and Shelley Chadwick
Mill Valley, California

(British couple felt anything possible in U.S.A.... start was minuscule, success was major... unknown strengths defined their jobs...both involved in hiring, resulting in outstanding staff... much growth...keep it simple and in its place)

The Chadwicks were educators in England, Michael a college professor and also a psychotherapist, and Shelley, a youth worker. The world of academia in England did not look particularly favorably on shopkeepers, so undoubtedly the Chadwicks would not have gone into business had they stayed in England.

In 1985 they visited the United States on an extended trip. They found there was an atmosphere of openness and encouragement toward business, that anything was possible. They wanted to stay.

Michael, through a family connection in England, had access to a line of thermal underwear that he felt would be unique in this country. But the Chadwicks had no capital.

However, Michael had observed the flea markets in the San Francisco Bay Area and felt that the thermal underwear could be sold through these outlets at different locations each weekend. They made the necessary arrangements, and a business was born! They began to generate income by selling at the flea markets, be it small at first.

The couple took sabbaticals from their work in England, and, for two years, Michael worked at a job in Berkeley, California, running an alternative junior high school. In 1987 he resigned, returned to England, sold their home and came back to settle in Marin County in the San Francisco Bay Area. Then they concentrated on properly launching their business.

Quite naturally the Chadwicks found that their marketing system, via flea markets, with its dependency on good weather, had its drawbacks. They stuck with it, however, as they moved forward in their retailing career. Incidentally, the flea markets' schedules made it necessary to get up at 2 in the morning to get in line for booth space for the day.

Next Michael and Shelley located a very suitable property in the beautiful town of Mill Valley, California, and launched their first lingerie store in May, 1988. (However, they also stayed with their flea markets for five years.) The Mill Valley shop made a profit from day one.

Both discovered that each of them brought clearly different strengths to the venture, strengths that they previously didn't know they possessed. That defined their jobs. In the beginning Shelley worked in the store and waited on the customers. She also did the buying, where she proved to have excellent taste. Michael manages the financial end of the business and seeks out new locations, which has led to a second store in San Anselmo, a neighboring town, and a third in San Francisco. They are proud of their outstanding staff, both of them being heavily involved with personnel selection. Now, Shelley works out of their home and Michael's office is over their San Francisco store. They have a daughter who comes first in their lives.

Like so many other successful couples in business together, both Michael and Shelley have proven that their relationship is strong enough to handle the ups and downs of their growing business. They make it a point, that even though their business is expanding, they strive to keep it simple and not to let the business take over their private life.

The Chadwicks' English friends can't figure out the couple's success. Simply put, the Chadwicks had a unique idea that, through patience, natural ability and very hard work, has become an established new business in a new country!

Doug and Dot Comm and their Dog, Rom™

© J&E Wyman 1999 World Rights Reserved

The Tennis Game

PRINTING

Sir Speedy
John and Sheri Statt
Scottsdale, Arizona

(Among Sir Speedy's top 25 stores...ownership and management moving from parents to the couple...great family approach to the business... three generations involved...staff of 40...now expanding with additional store)

Here is a franchising success story that rates high among all franchising success stories.

We're going to pick up the story at the time our married...in business couple, John and Sheri Statt, began working for Sheri's parents at their Sir Speedy printing operation in Scottsdale, Arizona.

John and Sheri had never met prior to John's going to work at the store in 1974, where Sheri had been working full time while still in high school.

At the time, John had been working for another printer, but was eager to move on to a greater career opportunity, particularly where he could work more hours. Recommended by his employer, John applied to Sheri's parents and was hired. At that time, John was engaged to be married.

One day Sheri noticed that John was shredding his wedding invitations. The engagement was off!

As John and Sheri worked together, they became truly best friends, not dating until a year after his engagement was broken. In 1979, they were married.

After their marriage, the couple continued in their careers at Sir Speedy, each moving naturally into his and her most effective areas of operation. John didn't enjoy management, but liked all aspects of selling and working with the company's outside sales force, where he excelled. Meanwhile, Sheri, who had worked at the store virtually all of her life, actually serving customers since she was 16, took on more and more of the total management responsibilities.

Today, Sheri is president of the company and oversees all aspects of the operation. Five team leaders, each of whom is responsible for a section of the business, report to Sheri. The store's staff now totals 40.

Expansion has always been a part of the family's plans, and currently, Sheri is directing the opening of a second store in north Scottsdale. She will now divide her time between the original downtown store and the new operation.

Sheri's dad is CEO of the firm, handling corporate and financial matters, plus long-range planning. Sheri's mother, who has also played a vital role, is still active in the company, but is cutting back due to health problems.

Gradually John and Sheri are taking over ownership of the firm, although Sheri has managed the business for the past 20 years. Their solid operations and current expansion is evidence that they have been doing an outstanding job.

It's interesting to note that John's former employer, who originally recommended him, is now working part time for the company.

As for the Statt's Sir Speedy store's mix of business, about 95 percent of their sales volume comes from printing work received from businesses, and about 5 percent from walk-in traffic.

The couple sing the praises of the Sir Speedy national franchising operation. They say that they get outstanding support from the corporation and are kept right up to date on the countless new developments that are continually breaking around them.

The feeling that the national organization has for the Statts and their operation must be mutual. Not only does this franchise hold the distinction of being the oldest in the system, the Statts receive on-going honors that include being appointed to special franchise boards. In addition John and Sheri have received the coveted Frannie Award from the Sir Speedy corporation, given to a husband and wife team in honor of their significant contribution to franchising and to their franchise network.

One grasps how busy and successful this couple has become. Tied right to all of their business activities is an enormous commitment to family. John and Sheri have two children who, as one can guess, have grown up with the business. In addition to working part time at the store, the children and their grandparents have accompanied John and Sheri to Sir Speedy national conventions, with the six of them traveling as a team.

When the Statt's children were very young, the grandparents, who live nearby, were able to help with transporting the children hither and yon to their many activities. This is indeed a model family, who work together in every way.

And that's not all. The Statts are very big on community service, too! In addition to teaching karate to youngsters, John is one of the organizers of a youth soccer program in north Scottsdale. In its three years of existence, the program has grown from just a few to its present 500 children.

Sheri has been president of the respected Scottsdale Leadership Program, which trains and prepares serious interested persons for future community service at the local and state level. Both of the Statts serve on their local high school boosters club, which vigorously supports the school's athletic activities.

John and Sheri believe strongly in the advantages of husbands and wives working together. They feel that it's a great plus to be married…in business, with both members working toward the same goal.

As would be expected, John and Sheri will continue to work hard for a long time in order to make possible an eventual normal transition over to their children if that proves to be the right thing for all.

There is a saying in marketing that all business is local. Here's a case that certainly bears that out. The extensive (now international) Sir Speedy franchising organization, with all of its facilities, systems and overview, has come to life in a very vibrant local manner with John and Sheri Statt's dynamic Scottsdale operation.

(www.sirspeedy.com)

Doug and Dot Comm and their Dog, Rom™

© J&E Wyman 1999 World Rights Reserved

The Cruise

Television and Appliances

Wheeler's TV & Appliances
Bob and Paula Wheeler
Damariscotta, Maine

(Successfully operated 70-year-old family business for 26 years...largest business in the area...try not to take it home, but she might be bookkeeping at four a.m...many hobbies, especially boating...they are very best friends)

Before we tell you about Bob and Paula Wheeler's busy business, we must tell you about their activities beyond their retail store.

The Wheelers are avid boaters. They live by a lake—the lake on which they met when they were children. Not only that, after they married, they honeymooned on a boat. To say that they love boating is an understatement.

Beyond all of this nautical activity, the Wheelers have hobbies galore! Paula quilts and Paula sews (she has nine sewing machines)—and Paula cooks and Paula gardens. In fact Paula admits to too many hobbies.

But wait, there's more. Bob is a fixer-upper. In fact the couple has built several houses (with their own hands), which they lived in then sold. Bob and Paula actually designed, engineered, constructed, wired and installed heat in these homes.

Their store is located in an old cow barn, which they remodeled. They installed a foundation under the barn, rebuilt it and put in rental spaces responsible for additional income.

How do they do it? As we indicated, their retail television and appliance store is very busy (they maintain a staff of six). To quote Bob in his conservative Maine manner, "We're very energetic people." Apparently so. And obviously they get along famously. They indicate that not only are they the very best of friends, they'd rather be with each other than with anybody else. Those are words that come from virtually every couple described in this book.

Now for their business, which has been in their family for over 70 years. Bob worked in the business from the time he was eight years old. Together, Bob and Paula have operated it for 26 years.

They divide up their duties, with Paula responsible for bookkeeping, the ordering of appliances, plus some sales work. Bob does most of the selling. He also handles repairs, often conducted in the customers' homes.

The Wheelers admit that dealing with the public presents a constant challenge. They are in an area of highly educated people, many computer literate, knowing all about prices from their excursions on the Internet. However, Bob and Paula are equal to the challenge. They belong to an association that lets them buy their merchandise very competitively, which, in turn, causes their prices to be competitive in the retail marketplace.

While eventually the Wheelers will retire and focus on their many hobbies, it would be difficult for them to leave their treasured five-acre property on the lake, where every day an eagle lands right on their lawn. Even during the winter months, beautiful evergreen trees give the area a much appreciated feel of greenery.

They colorfully describe a huge, fascinating mound composed of oyster shells that is less than a mile from their home. For over a hundred years, Indians came to this mound and shucked oysters until it was 80 to 90 feet high.

Bob and Paula have three grown children, every one of whom spent considerable time working at the store. Paula's mother also worked there for 15 years.

Paula good-naturedly indicates that poor Bob was surrounded by family with his wife, mother-in-law and children all working at the store. Actually, it speaks very well for this family that could work closely together as they continued a wonderful tradition.

Lighting, Decorating and Redecorating

Lights N' Such

Jerry and Anita LaFleiche
Powell, Wyoming

(Maintain compatibility of the marriage—give 90%, expect 40%...best friends...live in a small town offering hunting and fishing...make it fun...give great service and quality product... make sacrifices)

Here's the story of two delightful people who have been married for 38 years, and in business together for 19. They qualify to be in our top 20 percent in terms of length of time in business together, implying a lot of patience, a lot of love, real friendship and a great deal of business acumen! That's the LaFleiches through and through.

And they certainly qualify as a couple who picked the location of their business with their desired lifestyle clearly in mind. They had lived in Cheyenne, Wyoming, but wanted to move to a small town, one that could also offer retirement that definitely included hunting and fishing. Powell filled the bill. And they've never been sorry.

Jerry and Anita purchased what had been a home decorating business in Cheyenne, Wyoming, however it wasn't as developed as their present store. It was primarily a lighting business, which they have expanded to include window treatments and custom shower doors.

They purchased the business largely from their savings and went in relatively debt-free. They incorporated as a sub-chapter S corporation, and quickly selected the jobs that best suited each of them. Anita runs the store and designs lighting systems and drapery treatments for the customers. Jerry installs the draperies and shower doors, does the paperwork, and works on the computer.

Early on the LaFleiches faced the expected economic challenge. Competition came from Billings, Montana, but they learned that it could be met by providing outstanding service and a consistent, quality product. Jerry also stresses the great importance of listening to the customers and prioritizing their needs. "To compete, find your own niche and serve it well," he advises.

You may be sure that sacrifices are necessary to do the job properly, and Jerry and Anita have never shirked in this area. They advise that retail is not the place to expect to get rich quick; it takes long hours but includes a lot of satisfaction from a job well-done.

The LaFleiches approach their work with a good sense of humor, often teasing the customers. They feel that it is vital to have fun and enjoy one's work, thereby avoiding letting the business become a drag.

Jerry and Anita put the marriage relationship at the top of the list of important considerations for couples who are in business together. Jerry says, "The married couple who is in business together must work at maintaining the compatibility of the marriage without allowing the pressures of the business to get to them. There has to be a lot of give and take, with each one expecting to give 90 percent and expecting to take 40 percent!"

The couple agrees that they are most certainly great friends, but they also allow sufficient space apart from one another. In their case they do have separate activities, but certainly take trips together. Typically, they take extended weekends for vacations and sometimes take a week's vacation around Christmas—of course depending on the needs of the business.

In summary, the LaFleiches are convinced that any couple in business needs to care about each other, care about the customer, and care about the product. They are dedicated to the idea that you must have confidence in your product and be able to stand behind it.

Doug and Dot Comm and their Dog, Rom™

© J&E Wyman 1999 World Rights Reserved

The Fishing Trip

Awnings

Atlas Awning Company

Gordon and Mary Starr
Palm Springs, California

(Bought existing business...took five years to master it...deep love and friendship...very supportive...give each other room...have expanded lines of business...believe in a law of abundance)

Buying an existing business has its pluses. Usually the name of the business is established. Also, the existence of present customers gives the new owners a running start.

However, these advantages come with a price. Never should the new owners think that they won't have to work as hard as if they are starting a new business. Not only is there a lot to learn, but they must win over existing customers, while seeking new ones. Also there may be present employees to consider.

Gordon and Mary Starr's experience is a good example. After Gordon's career in construction ended, they purchased an existing awning business in Palm Springs, California. Previously Mary had been a computer programmer.

While today their business is successful, they explain that it took them five years to get a good handle on all of the aspects of the company. The transition for Gordon from working as a carpenter to operating a business that installed aluminum awnings was tremendous.

For one thing there were existing employees with whom to learn to communicate. As it happened, their first year was marked by a high turnover of help, so they also had to learn how to find the right new employees. Gordon states that their strong spiritual beliefs guided and sustained them during their challenging early years and have operated as a law of abundance for them.

Prior to purchasing the awning business, the Starrs lived in Los Angeles and later sold their house to use as startup capital for their new business enterprise in Palm Springs. Mary eventually came into the business, taking over all paperwork and bookkeeping. Gordon says that she is a natural at this, and she has since added the ordering of materials to her duties. Gordon handles sales, estimating and installation.

Presently they have seven employees, including one in office support, which allows Mary to spend quality time with their children.

The company has added a screen business to their basic work with awnings. At first Mary made the screens, but currently the office support assistant has taken over that operation. The couple are convinced that women build better screens because they have more patience than men.

It's interesting from a marketing standpoint that their original business primarily serviced mobile homes. However, Palm Springs isn't building any more mobile home parks, so in addition to working on the upkeep of existing mobile homes, they now also serve the needs of businesses.

Like so many couples who operate service businesses together, they consider word-of-mouth to be their primary advertising medium. They have found that satisfied customers do indeed spread the good word.

Both Gordon and Mary have kept a strong sense of humor throughout their years of operating their business. This was particularly necessary during their very challenging early years.

The Starrs say that sometimes things got so bad that the only thing that they could do was laugh!

They are grateful that their business is now well established and they've put aside all fear of failure. They state that they are very blessed in so many ways; first of all, with each other, with a rich home life, fine, happy children—with whom they are now able to take many vacations—and a flourishing business that they successfully operate together.

This certainly is a case where a couple purchased an existing business and worked every bit as hard as if it were a start-up operation. Their first five years of struggle has led to a sweet victory. Now they are carefully considering further expansion. The way the Starrs think and function, we won't be a bit surprised if that comes about.

Doug and Dot Comm and their Dog, Rom™

© J&E Wyman 1999 World Rights Reserved

Let's Advertise

French Restaurant

La Boheme

Alan and Kati Lewis
Carmel, California

(A 20-year success...paid off original loan in three years...unique approach to menu...regular clientele...consider mistakes learning experiences...much respect and trust...ability to compromise...family feeling with staff... community minded...yearly visit to France)

This was a marriage and business partnership that was meant to be. Prior to their marriage in 1976, Alan and Kati Lewis met when she was conference coordinator at a prominent Monterey County hotel and Alan was the maitre d'.

They laughingly tell of how they'd often butt heads when Kati set up her requirements and Alan had to follow her instructions. Somehow they worked through this. Next, Alan became restaurant manager at a luxury resort in the Big Sur area and Kati was invited to join the operation. At this point they began dating...and you know the rest.

After arranging for financing, in 1978, they purchased their present restaurant, which was more of a European restaurant at the time. They completely paid off their loan in three years.

Under the couple's ownership, the restaurant has evolved into a delightful French bistro that serves only one pre-scheduled entree each evening. The restaurant, which has family-style service, does not have a large kitchen and operates without a freezer.

Clearly, La Boheme presents a homey atmosphere that fits right into charming Carmel-by-the-Sea. It's no wonder that 50 to 60 percent of their business is from repeat customers.

However, it hasn't always been easy. At first they were both very young, just married and had no experience running their own restaurant. As a result they were quite jittery about their new business venture. They received much welcome encouragement from family and friends.

Of tremendous significance, the Lewises developed a great respect and trust for each other. They state that they learned to compromise and not expect to have everything go exactly the way one of them might want. Both Alan and Kati are vehement in saying that when a couple is in business together, there is no room for competition in either the marriage or the business. They also feel strongly that mistakes must be turned into learning experiences.

They promote their restaurant by publishing a regular calendar and have a presence on the Internet. By now they know most of their customers very well, and consider them and their staff to be their extended family.

Alan and the chef work very closely together in all aspects of food service. Kati hostesses, works on the menus and handles financial matters. Of course they both collaborate and make the major decisions together.

Be assured that, like most who are married…in business, the Lewises have faced and overcome adversity. At one point one of them had to virtually carry the business for the other. And now together they are reaping the rewards. They have earned their fine reputation and continued success.

As for advice to couples who are considering going into business together, they make the point that turns up so often in these profiles: that the couple must be best friends, share the same interests and values and give one another sufficient freedom to participate in desired activities. Kati, for example, is very involved in the local Carmel community.

Both Alan and Kati try not to take their business home with them, although they admit that it is always present.

A direct benefit of owning a French bistro is that the couple takes annual trips to France. This year they went to Europe for five weeks.

Hard work, knowing their business, dedication and an outstanding relationship through thick and thin have all contributed to the continuing success of Alan and Kati's La Boheme restaurant.

(www.laboheme.com)

INSURANCE

Kenneth L. Sawyer Insurance Brokers

Ken and Laura Sawyer
San Diego, California

(Strong love and appreciation…worked around the clock to make it go…overcame obstacles… paid back loan in one year…heavy participation in industry association…children relate to the business with own office space)

A romance developed at a San Diego insurance agency resulting in marriage in 1985 between Laura Autry, a former model, and Ken Sawyer, a young man bursting with ambition. Ken felt the insurance field offered the lifestyle he wanted. Their combined ambition led to their own business together three years later.

A client who was impressed with Ken had offered to help if he ever had a need. Now was the time, and he approached the client for a loan that would enable them to open their own insurance agency. The loyal client wrote the check and Ken and Laura found office space and set up shop. P.S.: They paid back the loan in one year!

The start was a bit rocky. On the Monday morning they planned to give notice to their employer, they found that their computer files had been erased, and they were shown the door.

Their employer had learned of their plans when their application for a bond for the new business was inadvertently sent to the soon-to-be former employer.

Undaunted, the Sawyers and two employees from the old agency set forth on their new venture. The first morning they found themselves in the new office with one phone in a closet, and three of them trying to use it.

Ken, with a natural love for sales, took over the vital selling responsibilities, backed up by Laura, who gravitated to the financial and administrative side. Today Laura, who eventually served a busy, successful term as president of the local independent agents' trade association, also jumps into sales work when necessary.

The couple's first major challenge came in their first year in business. They opened their doors in April of 1988, and in the fall a statewide law, Proposition 103, was passed that negatively impacted the insurance brokerage business.

So here they were, a new business, a new home, a small child, and a changing business climate. At times they wondered what they were doing!

However, they constantly buoyed each other up. Coming home at night, each knew the challenges the other had faced that day and each helped the other gear up for the next day. Ken vowed to work from six in the morning until ten at night if that's what it took. Be assured that they did fulfill the needs of the business, and today have built a successful insurance agency.

The Sawyers were fortunate to have two sets of grandparents available in the area to help with their two children. Eventually the children were given their very own office in the agency to use as a headquarters. At ages nine and 12, they often help out, making photo copies, faxing and collating, plus handling other suitable tasks. Ken and Laura have always been able to arrange their schedules to be available for the children's activities.

Looking back at their start in business, Ken eagerly admits that a major motivation to being in business together was that he was so in love with Laura that he wanted to be with her all the time! Further, each had been successful in their prior careers, so they felt confident that they would work well together, especially since their abilities complemented each other.

The Sawyers are a couple who have built their marriage and their business on a strong foundation. It's no wonder they are succeeding!

Doug and Dot Comm and their Dog, Rom™

© J&E Wyman 1999 World Rights Reserved

Wearing More Than One Hat

INVESTMENT SERVICES

McMichael & Associates

Jim and Irby McMichael
Sausalito, California

(In the right business with the right division of duties...only one can be quarterback...totally committed...win with personal service... establish budgets, goals and projections...settle disagreements quickly)

First, some background: Jim McMichael, a classic entrepreneur, was a partner in a small investment firm in San Diego, having previously established and sold three other businesses. Irby held a very responsible position with a venture capital company handling real estate development projects. Both excelled in their work.

Seeking wider horizons, Jim was ready for a change, and at the same time Irby became disenchanted with her work. Her challenging involvement in the construction of apartment houses and shopping centers had slowed down with the real estate market in California.

The time was now right for the couple to seek a new experience together. Their era of teaming up was about to begin—in steps. First, they left San Diego and moved to a small town on the central coast of California. Here, they went to work together for a large stock brokerage firm, where Jim became impressed with a product offered to his firm by an investment company that he felt was very meritorious. However, he was convinced that the company was doing a poor job in marketing the product.

Next move? Jim and Irby convinced the investment firm that they could better represent them and more effectively market their service to retail brokerages as a wholesaler, working as an outside contractor.

And the investment company bought the idea! The McMichaels organized, set up their marketing office plans—and cast their eyes up toward the San Francisco Bay Area.

Jim and Irby are an excellent example of a couple working together who adjusted their business location to their desired lifestyle. They moved north, to beautiful Sausalito, California. Here, they leased an attractive, nicely furnished houseboat to serve as their office.

Of great importance, they established a very efficient division of duties, working in the areas in which each excels. Jim, having been a quarterback playing football during his school days admits to needing to be the quarterback—feeling strongly that only one person can take ultimate responsibility for the business. Obviously Jim is qualified by his experience and license to sell the investment service, while Irby's background allows her to handle all of the vital accounting and organizational activities. He is the creative partner, and Irby, the professional business expert.

Irby efficiently and effectively handles administration, including income and expense projections, goals and budgets. She admits to feeling very fulfilled in this business venture with Jim. She loves the business and is extremely happy knowing that it belongs to them.

Do they have disagreements? Certainly. However, they've worked it out so that each always presents his or her point of view. Then they see to it that the disagreement is over in a matter of minutes because they always keep the big picture in mind.

Jim is the type of entrepreneur who, when he has decided to start a business, has been willing to change the whole pattern of his life to accommodate it. With the extremely able Irby at his side, he knows no fear about the future of the business.

As for advice to couples planning to go into business together, Jim says, "First make sure that it is a good business, and then totally commit yourselves to making it successful." He continues, "If you are operating a small business that competes with the big boys, then give the best possible personal service. You can probably beat them in that department!"

A good point for all couples in small businesses to heed!

Doug and Dot Comm and their Dog, Rom™

© J&E Wyman 1999 World Rights Reserved

True Love…A Married in Business Advantage

Piano Studio

Bronson Studio

Lynwood and Renee Bronson
Carmel, California

(Identical goals...triumphed through years of education and part-time jobs...ultimately realized their dream...found unique niche in broadened approach to music education...gave their art a solid business foundation)

Lyn and Renee Bronson are more than just piano teachers. They are musical educators in a broader-than-usual sense. They offer a deep approach to piano instruction and are a significant part of their community's respected music scene, producing many concerts.

And the Bronsons are partners in every sense of the word. They have worked out their life together so that they share both professional and personal responsibilities and duties in a way that is conducive to the well-being of each. Noteworthy is Lyn's aim to take as much of the household duties as possible off of Renee so that she can spend most of her time at the Steinway.

Of course teaching (and forever practicing) is their primary activity, and they both put that first. In addition, Lyn is the computer expert, handling business matters, including their public relations needs. He uses the computer's desktop publishing capability, designing business forms, stationery, flyers and studio brochures. Renee pays the bills and manages personal household accounts. Their accountant has taught them to keep their books in order and to generate regular profit and loss statements.

By professionally teaming up, the Bronsons have given their students the solid foundation of two richly educated, trained and experienced musicians, with the underpinning of their well-structured business.

But this didn't just happen. As an inspiration to other couples who are striving for their dream to come true, it would be well to glance at Lyn and Renee's struggle to bring about their ultimately achieved goal. They worked hard and long over many years to begin their careers in music.

The Bronsons were married in 1961. Renee met Lyn when he was in the U.S. Army and stationed in Europe. From that time on they had many challenging years during which they worked at various jobs to maintain themselves while they lived with their goal.

They both went from part-time job to part-time job—Lyn in retail stores, sometimes on his feet for 12 hours a day, and Renee in restaurants—where once she was forced into cooking though she didn't know how. Lyn learned piano tuning, which at least kept him involved with music.

However, the Bronsons never lost sight of their dream. During these years they developed ambitious ideas about how their partnership would function.

Finally, Lyn and Renee made the break, moved to Carmel and set up in business. Even then they took part-time jobs while they endeavored to start a piano-teaching studio.

To introduce themselves, they produced a small flyer that included a photograph of the two of them at the piano. This showed that they were reasonably young and very presentable. The flyer listed their training and experience and indicated that they had relocated from the Los Angeles area.

They sent the flyer to every school and college in the area. In addition, they sent one to all of their competitors with an accompanying letter asking them to "send us crumbs from your table and we would be most grateful." They made the point that they would even welcome difficult students.

Within a few weeks they had several students—not enough to support their studio, but it was a start. During that first year Lyn and Renee also volunteered to play mini recitals at retirement homes and convalescent hospitals. This brought recognition as some of these events received press coverage.

Next they were invited to join the board of directors of the prestigious Carmel Music Society. Eventually Lyn was invited to join the board of the Monterey County Symphony.

Within a year they were able to quit their part-time jobs and the ultimate success of the Bronson Studio was assured.

As to their teaching policies: Their plan of instruction is based on music fundamentals for beginning and intermediate students and professional training for the more advanced.

The Bronsons have gone far beyond just providing piano lessons with occasional recitals. They offer preparation for competitive auditions, which could be a launching pad for those with the motivation and mental toughness to perform. Performance classes are held every other week.

As previously stated, Lyn and Renee are a real team. Often one will be teaching in the upstairs studio while the other practices downstairs. They enjoy a daily luncheon where they have their official update meetings. They admit to having occasional arguments, but more often than not these are over which movie to see or to which restaurant they should go for lunch.

Lyn and Renee Bronson have realized their ambitions, married…in business; now they're helping others to realize theirs.

(www.bronsonpianostudio.com)

Driver Training

Miller Driving School

Greg and Misty James
Palm Springs, California

(Young, affirmative couple took over family business... learned it...financed it...expanded it...are succeeding with it...settle disagreements by compromise...show the necessary patience and calm needed by their students)

Here's a bright, happy young couple living and conducting their business in one of America's beauty spots, Palm Springs, California. They're realizing their ambition to operate their own company together. They enjoy their work and are succeeding with it. Why wouldn't Greg and Misty James be affirmative about their business and their lifestyle? And they are!

Misty's grandfather started the Miller Driving School in 1974. From there the business went to Misty's aunt, who moved it to Cotati, California, in 1984. In 1994, seizing on what appeared to them to be a real opportunity, Greg and Misty purchased the Miller Driving School name and reopened the school in their home. They had already determined that they didn't want to work for anyone else, so the timing seemed right.

With California's law requiring everyone under 18 to take driver's education plus six hours of actual driving training prior to receiving an operator's license, Greg and Misty saw a bright potential for the business, which already had a well-established name.

Previously Greg spent six years in the Marine Corps and felt that he'd had good experience in organizing and setting up systems, an attribute Misty teasingly questions but goes along with.

Incidentally, the very affirmative young couple believes in compromising differences, rather than holding firmly to a strong controversial stand.

After the Jameses purchased the school, they obtained the necessary forms from the Department of Motor Vehicles, enrolled in and completed the necessary classes that qualified them for teaching. Some financing was necessary, as they had to purchase furniture for their home-based business, plus two vehicles for student driving.

An efficient and harmonious division of duties evolved right from the beginning, with Misty teaching driver's education in the classroom. She also made appointments and kept the books.

At the start, classes were held on weekends. Both Greg and Misty took students during the week for driving instruction.

Of course, a business such as a driving school must promote itself to become known in the community. In this regard, Greg goes to the schools and teaches classes. They also advertise in the yellow pages and do some couponing.

Things have now evolved so that Greg and his brother handle the driving instruction. Misty will get back to that as soon as they purchase an additional car for that purpose.

A great advantage of the James's home-based business is that Misty can easily care for their two small children.

Greg and Misty have developed a very solid philosophy regarding their teaching of the young people who are learning to drive. They feel that the key to successful driver instruction is to keep calm so that the teenagers feel reassured. Quite naturally the couple expects the students to make mistakes, but when that happens, they matter-of-factly review what the student should have done differently.

Frequently the problem occurs as a result of other drivers. When that happens, they'll ask for the student's assessment of what the other driver should have done, and of course, the student learns from this.

To the Jameses their reputation means everything. Happily, theirs appears to be excellent, as a high percentage of their students pass the DMV test the first time around.

Greg and Misty James were smart enough to seize upon a good opportunity when it came along, and have made the most of it!

Doug and Dot Comm and their Dog, Rom™

© J&E Wyman 1999 World Rights Reserved

Cleaning Day at the Home-based Office

Picture Framing—Fine Art

The Painters Place

Stan and Pat Painter
Larkspur, California
San Francisco, California

(On-going learning...finding and perfecting their niche...research...loving their business... expanding it into their family...best friends... no ego...no bickering)

Thirty-two years ago, in 1966, congenial Stan Painter took a deep breath and made the leap. He left his secure job at a large San Francisco advertising agency because he wanted to be in a business where his great love of painting fine art would fit.

Teaming up with his able and versatile wife, Pat, they bought a store in Marin County's picturesque Larkspur, California. The store had been selling paint, wall-paper and art supplies. Here is another case where the physical location offered a much sought after lifestyle, at the same time becoming the business opportunity the entrepreneurial couple were seeking. And they could do it together!

At first Pat worked on the books at home, since they had four small children, while Stan worked in the store. As the children grew up, Pat spent more time in the store, where she became curious about framing. She wanted to know all about it, so she talked to suppliers and sales representatives. However, they weren't very knowledgeable. She tried to talk to museum people, but they kept the information to themselves, as they felt picture framers ruined the art.

In 1970 the Professional Picture Framers Association was formed with Stan and Pat as charter members. The association was made up of framers, suppliers to the trade and others who knew the museum techniques. The members shared their information and taught each other what they knew.

Along with this development, in 1971 the Painters moved their store, and eventually gave up the paint, wallpaper and art supplies aspects of their business and concentrated on their true love, custom picture framing. And the business moved forward.

Meanwhile Stan began spending one day a week at home painting. By 1979 they began selling his paintings in the store, where it became an important aspect of their success. As the years progressed Stan has spent more time painting and less in the store.

Meanwhile Pat learned to handle all phases of the framing operation, even hand-cutting mats, until they bought a machine for that function. Pat's forte is working with the customers; she truly loves the challenge of helping make the right choice of frames.

In 1978 the Painters purchased another store, this one in San Francisco. Their existing inventory included wonderful old-time mouldings from the 1920s. Their eldest son, Matt, ultimately joined them in their San Francisco location. At first he was particularly interested in the old mouldings. Ultimately he expanded his interests and successfully worked on the entire business of the store.

Today, Matt, now a Certified Picture Framer, has become the titular head of both the San Francisco and Larkspur stores. However, be assured that his parents are still very involved in the Larkspur location, still a team!

Asked about advice for couples in business, both Stan and Pat emphasize that a couple in business must really like each other. They should not compete with each other or be critical about every little thing. Bickering should be avoided.

It's interesting to note that when the Painters get together for family dinners (still another son has come into the business), spirited brainstorming sessions are sure to follow.

And be happy for Stan. Now he paints every day and can be found in the store only on Saturdays—where he may be seen vacuuming!

Doug and Dot Comm and their Dog, Rom™

© J&E Wyman 1999 World Rights Reserved

Night at the Movies

Dentistry + Inn + Apartment Complex

Coachman's Inn

Gordon and Sandy Steuck
Carmel, California

(From Los Angeles to Carmel...branched out beyond his dental profession and her nursing... teamed up into also owning and operating flourishing inn plus an apartment complex... strong marriage brings healthy attitudes to expanding businesses...exciting hobbies)

Gordon and Sandy Steuck are a handsome couple who will always appear to be youthful due to their bright, enthusiastic outlook on both their business and their life. They have kept Gordon's specialized dental profession active and have added exciting new business ventures to their lives.

The Steucks were living in Los Angeles, having married in 1968. Gordon was an endodontist and Sandy, a nurse. They made frequent trips to beautiful Carmel-by-the Sea, an area they learned to love. Visiting with many dentists in Carmel, Gordon was encouraged by them to move there since there were no endodontists.

So the couple made their move. They knew that they had a strong marriage and could harmoniously and successfully include the operation of a business.

Gordon set up his dental office, and soon they bought a 43-unit apartment complex. Later, they purchased the Coachman's Inn, a delightful establishment.

The couple's organizational methods and division of work are interesting. Previously Sandy, as a nurse, had no business experience. But she was a natural! She began by noticing that Gordon was spending too many evenings writing out their checks at bill-paying time. So she took over in order to allow the couple to spend their evenings together. That led to Sandy taking over the paper work including bill-paying for all three of their businesses.

However, Sandy is responsible for much more than that. The individual managers at the Coachman's Inn and at the apartment complex report to her. She also handles the administrative side of Gordon's dental practice.

Sandy follows through with initial implementation of innovative Gordon's many expansive ideas. For example, if Gordon had an idea for expanding the Coachman's Inn, it would become Sandy's job to work with their architect, contact City Hall, and follow through on the myriad details inherent in the project. If it was determined that the project was do-able, Gordon then would step in.

Sandy oversees construction work, bringing Gordon back in at key times, especially when problems develop. To his credit, Gordon makes it a point to consult with experienced, successful business people, feeling that he can always learn from them.

Yes, Gordon and Sandy Steuck are glad that they moved to Carmel where they really wanted to live. Better still is that they found a way that Gordon can keep his specialized profession active, while he is teamed up with Sandy to expand their business interests.

Who's in charge of this busy, creative team? Though they work together very closely, Sandy says, ultimately one person needs to be the boss—and she says, "Gordon is it! I'm happy to be his partner!"

Incidentally, Gordon is a man of many talents and interests. His hobbies include collecting and working on vintage automobiles, and he flies his own airplane.

It's very clear that Gordon and Sandy Steuck were bound to become entrepreneurial and enter businesses beyond their original professions. Their move to Carmel shows the adventuresome spirit so common with couples who are married...in business.

Heating and Air Conditioning

Abercrombie Air Systems

Steve and Deedra Abercrombie
Palm Springs, California

(Sought to better themselves from past jobs in a gratifying activity...difficult at first...required faith, dedication, diligence...the business became their niche in life...ultimately it took hold)

A strong motivation brought the Abercrombies into a business of their own. Married in 1982 and living in Southern California, Steve drove a truck and Deedra worked at a prominent retail store. Two years later the couple found themselves wanting a better life both for their family and for each other. At the same time they wanted to spend their time doing something that was fulfilling and gratifying.

Following their dreams they launched forth in the air conditioning business. At one time Steve had worked for his father, who owned a radiator repair business, so he knew the basics of air conditioning. They decided that air conditioning would be their field and opened for business in Cucamonga, California.

Working at first out of their home, Deedra answered the phones, handled all scheduling and dispatching, plus the paperwork.

Steve, of course, moved right into doing the actual repair work for the customers. They experimented with some yellow page advertising, but soon found that word-of-mouth was the most effective way for them to promote their business.

They really didn't formalize goals at the start. After getting underway (and it was difficult at first, with many sleepless nights), the goals began to shape themselves. From the beginning Steve and Deedra, in addition to their good motives, had a strong faith in God, in their family, in one another and in life itself. They are grateful to their family for aiding in the creation of their business. The family helped to run the household and rented a home to them at low cost.

Be assured that the Abercrombies remained extremely diligent in their all-out attempt to make the business work. After two years they acquired a warehouse in Ontario, California, planning to ultimately move to Palm Springs, where they wanted to live.

It is interesting to note that when they made the actual move to Palm Springs their business was still in Ontario, resulting in a 70-mile (each way) commute. This added stress to the entire relationship, something that the Abercrombies definitely didn't want. So they reassessed what was most important to them and started the business all over again in Palm Springs in 1989.

After one year in Palm Springs, the business picked up and they were on their way to a successful operation.

The Abercrombies, when asked to give advice to other couples, responded with some very good pointers. Steve said, "Make sure that the business is your niche in life. Be dedicated to the right things. Don't be in it just for the money...save money in advance...learn computers, and be sure to give each other space!"

Deedra said, "Each person should be assigned areas of duties at which he or she is good and really interested. Find your gift and offer it to the business. Grow from there."

Deedra also emphasized the necessity of giving each other sufficient space. She said, "Turmoil is created in tight situations. Neither party should cross the other's positions."

The Abercrombies' faith, dedication and diligence brought success!

Doug and Dot Comm and their Dog, Rom™

© J&E Wyman 1999 World Rights Reserved

The Pitch to Buy the Business

CHIROPRACTIC OFFICES

Dr. William M. Baeza

Bill and Bernice Baeza
Mill Valley, California

(Both partners excel in their individual areas... no overlapping...each respects and honors the other's viewpoint...an unusually professionally run office...now expanding via more family in the firm)

Bill and Bernice Baeza represent a marriage partnership that carries over perfectly into their business partnership. Each has a very definite role in which each excels. Both respect, trust and support the other's areas of operation.

On the very rare occasions when they have differences of opinion on significant policy matters, the Baezas acknowledge the other's viewpoint and find a satisfactory compromise that results in a solid decision.

For six years prior to his marriage to Bernice, Bill worked with a group of chiropractors in San Francisco. In 1979 he desired to open his own office in the beautiful town of Mill Valley, California. (Again, a delightful lifestyle choice made by a couple running their own business.)

And yes, Bill wanted his new bride to team up with him in operating his office. Bernice, who had previously owned her own motorcycle dealership, ultimately agreed, bringing excellent administrative, management and marketing skills to her new position.

Of course, Bill was only too delighted to completely turn those functions over to Bernice. Indicative of how she was needed, she discovered Bill's unique bookkeeping—two boxes, one marked "to be paid," the other marked "already paid." That was it. Bernice soon transformed the informality into what became a fine-tuned, professionally run office.

Of course, the couple's natural breakdown of duties was obvious. Bill was now able to devote his time to his professional endeavors, primarily his diagnostic work, plus many talks and lectures on his subject.

Bill is also glad that Bernice, who is in charge of personnel, is there to handle the sticky "people" problems that come up in every business. Of course this makes it possible for Bill to focus on his primary responsibilities, which are, after all, the reason for their business.

Bernice is quick to tell of her complete confidence in Bill's consistently outstanding performance in his areas of responsibility. What's more, Bernice says, "Bill's easy to work for, he keeps a good schedule and gets to work on time!"

Here's a husband and wife in business together where the division of duties call forth both of their very excellent backgrounds of proven abilities. Together, they effectively offer the best of their former worlds of experience.

It's interesting to note that the Baeza children have played an important part in the operation. Naturally, as with most small family businesses, the children are very much exposed to the family business. Once when one of their daughters was very young, she presented her parents with a common tearful complaint that they talked business too much around the home. This caused the parents to try to bring more balance into their daughters' lives.

Nevertheless, the Baezas firmly believe that family businesses can provide a good foundation for their offspring. In this case it has certainly worked out that way. Both of the Baeza daughters worked in the business while in college, much to the advantage of all.

The Baezas are proud to tell that one of their daughters is now a licensed chiropractor working in their business.

Here's a couple who obviously have a great deal of respect for each other's abilities. It is a respect that shows in all aspects of their smoothly operating, professionally run office. Their chosen beautiful Mill Valley, California, lifestyle offers another big plus to their endeavor.

Doug and Dot Comm and their Dog, Rom™

© J&E Wyman 1999 World Rights Reserved

Luncheon Confession

Hair Replacement

Tony Martingilio, Inc.

Tony and Karen Martingilio
Scottsdale, Arizona

(Truly best friends...an affirmative, positive attitude...individual responsibilities that don't overlap... fortitude...an understanding, caring approach to each other and to their customers—in a sensitive business)

When you walk into the fresh, clean atmosphere of Tony and Karen Martingilio's hair replacement establishment in Scottsdale, the tasteful works of art that adorn the walls, the sounds of laughter and the busy telephone speak of a successful business. It is a business that doesn't even hint of the embarrassment new customers bring with them into a hair replacement facility. Here you're greeted by the joyous smile and upbeat welcome of outgoing, petite Karen, and you begin to understand the obvious success of the couple who own and operate this business.

Full of energy and the very personification of an affirmative attitude, Karen sets the stage for the loyal clientele being served by their staff. Enter tall, husky, jovial Tony, whose voice immediately fills the room. You observe that Tony approaches his business with a combination of vigor and artistic creativity.

Actually, Tony began his career as a commercial artist in Chicago. When he personally needed a hairpiece, he decided to change his career and go to work for the man who designed and supplied it. His new employer, concerned that in the past employees had learned from him and then departed to start their own businesses, taught Tony nothing!

This didn't stop the determined, young would-be entrepreneur, who studied, observed and, in time, had the confidence to start his own hair replacement service. Eventually, he built a fine business in Chicago, given an enormous leap forward by a featured appearance on the popular Phil Donahue television show.

However, soon after they were married about 15 years ago, the Martingilios left their lucrative hair replacement business in Chicago to move to Scottsdale, Arizona, where they wanted to live and work (typical of the lifestyle choices made by so many couples who are in business together).

The Scottsdale market turned out to be very different, especially for Tony. They were unknown in the area and the customers stayed away in droves.

Happily, Karen's encouraging and consistently optimistic view prevailed. They hung on and began to advertise.

But it took time for the advertising to produce. The first month brought no response. The second month again, zero! The third month, finally a call! They kept at it and ultimately their business became firmly established.

Indicative of how the Martingilios function as a couple is this quote from Karen: "Being in business together, a couple needs to approach their work on the same fundamental basis. They need to share the same positive, affirmative philosophy, the same vision of what life should be. In addition to having a strong marriage, they should be best friends!"

Karen continues: "A positive attitude brings positive energy, and that's catching. We've seen it result in calls and business rolling in!"

Tony speaks of Karen as a very honest, caring person who respects his talent and, at the same time, truly understands the clients' fears and concerns in dealing with the sensitive subject of hair replacement.

As far as how they handle the difficult days, the Martingilios understand each other so well that each knows when to give the other space. On the other hand, a good day often means going out to dinner to celebrate. Incidentally, they have a rule to never talk about negative things during dinner—only positive!

Here's a couple, married…in business, making it work in a sensitive field where an affirmative attitude brings tangible results.

Doug and Dot Comm and their Dog, Rom™

© J&E Wyman 1999 World Rights Reserved

The New Car

Gift Shop

Seven Seas

Bruce and Olive Grimes
Carmel, California

(The desired lifestyle drove the purchase of the business, which lasted 40 years...the store and Carmel's music scene became their life...two giving people totally supportive of the community and each other)

Bruce and Olive Grimes were married for 46 years, and they spent 40 of them in business together in one of America's most beautiful areas, Carmel-by-the-Sea on California's Monterey Peninsula. They owned and operated a lovely gift shop, Seven Seas, in the heart of downtown Carmel, where one could always find either Bruce or Olive—or both—presenting their personally selected merchandise to the public.

Their 40 years in business together qualifies the Grimes as "the couple featured in this book with the most years spent married...in business."

They were wonderful, sometimes challenging, always happy, productive years, spent serving a regular clientele who came from far and wide to shop at Seven Seas and visit with the Grimes.

Bruce had worked for an advertising agency in San Francisco, commuting to his home in Palo Alto, where his wife, Olive, was a homemaker and full-time mother of son, John. The time came for a change of business scene, and the couple took stock of what they really wanted. They both loved picturesque Carmel, with its ocean, pine trees, crooked streets, unique shops and emphasis on fine art and classical music. In fact they had looked forward to retiring there someday.

At the suggestion of Olive's mother, the couple spent a weekend in Carmel just to see if a business might be for sale that they would enjoy owning and operating. And there was! And they bought it! And they operated it for 40 years! (Testimony to the fact that they enjoyed it!)

Their first location was in a charming, little courtyard, graced by a lush, beautiful fuchsia plant, where they ate their lunch each day. However, quoting Olive, "But you don't go into business to go out under the fuchsia to eat your lunch!" Two-and-a-half years later they moved to a better location.

A memorable point in those early days of their business is that neither of the Grimes ever believed they could fail. They never even considered it. Also noteworthy is their statement, "We can never have a divorce in our family, because neither of us would want to run the store alone!"

They started their business with $2,500 worth of merchandise, with both of them involved in the buying. They began business featuring imports exclusively, but were stuck when a New York dock strike disastrously held up their orders. From that time on they added domestic resources—resulting in about a 50-50 division of goods.

Olive's sunny, outgoing personality made it natural for her to handle most of the waiting on the trade, while Bruce did the building of fixtures, the special wrapping of fragile gifts, the shipping, the bookkeeping and, of course, he also helped the customers.

They found that more and more they were sending customers to a card store for gift cards, when an idea hit. Why not build a special card display and offer lovely gift cards for sale themselves? They did it and found a new profitable product. They built a reputation for having the best card selection in town.

Ask the classical music community about the Grimes and they will emote with operatic fervor about both of their contributions, particularly to the Carmel Bach Festival. It was here that Bruce, who had been an opera singer in years gone by, became the first local professional to join the chorale at the annual Bach Festival. He also served on the Carmel Music Society board of directors. Both served on the Chamber Music Society board, each chairing its national competition for chamber music groups.

After 40 wonderful, productive years of tenderly caring for each other and for their business and their community, the Grimes retired. And they are missed!

Restaurant and Bar

Paul and Robin
A seashore town

(First, a success then problems)

Here's the story of a couple who were married and in business together, and sadly, though their business succeeded, the marriage didn't. Through hard work and intensive learning over a period of ten years, they had achieved success. And then something went very wrong. Our purpose in relating this story is to point up the problem and let it serve as a vivid example to other couples. Perhaps it will help someone else take the necessary steps that could avoid the same mistake.

The names we use are fictitious, but real people were indeed involved. Paul and Robin were a bright, good-looking, young couple, living in the Northwest. When their story begins the couple felt that they could make a better living if they owned their own business. They sold their home and moved to a delightful area that we'll just call a seashore town in another state.

With $10,000 in the bank, they went to a business broker and gave him their criteria. They were willing to go into any business they could learn. They wanted to be near the ocean, and the purchase could even be the result of a distress sale. Ultimately, they bought a restaurant and bar in their desired location from owners who were eager to sell and agreed to hold the paper. The couple had very little money, no credit and no financing help. The purchase agreement held that the previous owners would teach the young couple the business, beginning the day the transaction was completed, but alas, the former owners were gone, out of sight! The couple called the business broker in panic and wanted out of the deal. Not possible. There they were with a business to learn and operate!

As you can imagine, they went to work around the clock, each on a twelve-hour shift. Robin cooked, tended bar, even cleaned the toilets. At 2 a.m., Paul came to work, remodeling, popping out windows, thereby making an open-air bar, pushing out walls, converting a bathroom into a kitchen, cleaning up, and in the daytime, dealing with the local bureaucracy.

This schedule went on for four years, at which time they paid off their balloon payment. After six years the couple felt that they had a successful operation. So they purchased a second restaurant around the corner.

In actuality Paul and Robin raised the standard of the two restaurants, both as to atmosphere and clientele. They became well liked in the neighborhood and in the community. At one point they sold the second restaurant and concentrated on their first endeavor.

As their volume grew Robin continued to run the kitchen and trained the cooks and waitresses, while Paul handled all of the administrative work.

Things seemed to be going very well. The couple had worked unbelievably hard, learned the business, upgraded the operation, which certainly could be considered successful. And then it happened.

After ten years in business together, problems took over the marriage. A divorce followed, and that was that. For the next five years Robin operated the restaurant by herself, paying Paul for his share of the business.

With an unbelievably heavy schedule and no vacation in sight, Robin sought a partner. She was unsuccessful in finding the right one. Meanwhile, she began to feel that with her proven skills, she could make as good a living working for someone else. It's easy to see how, at this point, she could tire of the whole thing.

So, Robin took the step and sold the business outright.

Today she feels that she made a big mistake in selling out. She discovered that other restaurants considered her to be overqualified for openings that they had. With no college degree, no certification and not a very broad business experience, Robin has found it difficult to land a position that would pay her enough to maintain her established standard of living.

Now, to point up the lesson from this sad story. Here were two bright, hard-working, innovative, attractive people who had created a true business success. What went wrong?

Robin says that it's simple: She and Paul just didn't give enough thought or time to their marriage. Now she realizes that they should have taken time for each other. They should have kept their marriage fresh. Perhaps taking a number of short vacations would have helped, as well as regular dinner dates together, and maybe the theater. They really needed to think about each other.

We hope the readers of this book will take heed!

Doug and Dot Comm and their Dog, Rom™

© J&E Wyman 1999 World Rights Reserved

The Plan for Succession

PLUMBING + CONSTRUCTION + ENTREPRENEURIAL VENTURES

(Gas Station, Ice Cream Shop, Motel & More in Illinois, to Hardware Store in Florida)

Alcon to Rand Motel to Johnson's Hardware

Alvin & Connie Johnson

Lake Zurich, Illinois, then Marathon, Florida

(Plumber by trade, adventuresome entrepreneurs by choice...when plumbing business slowed, started several new businesses...ultimately a successful motel...then realized dream of hardware store in Florida)

This is a story of a couple, Al and Connie Johnson, who, if anybody ever did, epitomize the pioneer spirit that built our nation.

Through thick and thin they stuck together and kept plowing forward, working hard at each venture. When things were more than tough during the Depression, they scratched their way to survival and ultimately enjoyed a great victory, the realization of a dream come true.

It starts out as the story of a man who loved and learned the plumbing trade in Chicago. He married his Connie who turned out to be the one in a million. She could keep pace with his ideas and work, work, work, always helping her husband's dreams come to fruition.

It wasn't easy. And it didn't happen quickly.

Al didn't want to work in a plumbing shop in Chicago, so the couple moved out to the country. Together they built a home in the Lake Zurich rural area about 25 miles from Chicago on a main highway.

Al took on the plumbing jobs that came his way and Connie handled the ordering of plumbing supplies, followed-up on deliveries and took care of paper work.

The demand for plumbing work felt the effect of the big Depression and this made it difficult, since the couple now also had a very young daughter.

The Johnsons knew they had to do something about the situation, so they installed a gas station on their property. Next, Al put in an ice cream and sandwich shop.

As for Connie, she manned the gas pumps, served sandwiches and ice cream and backed up Al with whatever he needed for his plumbing business. Once Al called Connie from a job saying that he needed a certain valve and couldn't wait for the supply truck to deliver it. So Connie drove to Chicago to pick it up. It turned out not to be the right valve, so off Connie went again on a second 50-mile-round-trip errand.

Then there was the time that Al had an idea that raising chickens would supplement their income, so he built a chicken coup and bought the chickens. More for Connie to do! It was her task to feed the chickens and collect the eggs. Here was a job that could also be handled by the Johnson's little girl. Wrong! After she dropped and broke two dozen eggs that she had just collected, she was relieved of that duty! The chicken endeavor ended badly as the flock became infected and many of them died. Enough with the chickens.

Alvin took the vacated chicken space and went to work. He built three small, two-room apartments, closed the gas station and expanded the ice cream and sandwich shop. Next he built five tourist rooms and continued to add facilities to their property, and with it, additional businesses.

Yes, Connie continued to be the uncomplaining partner who was instrumental in making Al's ideas succeed. Of course, through it all, Al continued to service his plumbing business, so he also worked very hard.

Next the couple purchased nearby property with the intention of building and operating a motel. They sold their first home, land and its various businesses, and moved into the house on the new property.

Then began several years of construction. They remodeled the house into two apartments, and Al, again with Connie's help and encouragement, built 12 motel units, four two-room apartments and a large motel office with living quarters.

The motel proved to be the Johnson's most successful endeavor and Al kept busy with the maintenance work. Now Connie was the busiest that she'd ever been. In order to run the operation at a profit, the Johnsons didn't even consider hiring additional help.

Connie would strip the beds as soon as the first units were empty, usually at five o'clock in the morning. She did all of the laundry herself, using an old wringer-type washing machine. Then came the outside clothesline for drying. In the evenings Connie would iron the bed linen between registering guests.

By now that little girl who had dropped the collected eggs, had gone off to college, married and was living in Southern California, and had two little daughters of her own. However, as things worked out, she returned to Lake Zurich as a single mother. She and her girls were warmly welcomed by her parents.

The daughter applied for and got a job, but tried to help her mother with the enormous workload, which boggled the daughter.

On one occasion Connie and her daughter were getting an apartment ready for a new tenant. The two of them were washing the walls. The daughter couldn't keep up with her mother and wished they could both stop. Not on your life! Connie had a job to do and was definitely going to get it done!

Now for the couple's ultimate dream.

Shortly after Al and Connie were married, they greatly enjoyed a brief stay in Florida. And the dream began. Al, especially, had his heart set on someday living and having a business in Florida.

Yes, it happened. The Johnsons were able to make a trade—their motel for a hardware store located on Marathon Key in South Florida.

Al was in his glory. They were owners of a home, a hardware store and a small motor boat. They both worked in the store and thoroughly enjoyed finally being in Florida.

Some two years later, a hurricane hit the area and Al and Connie evacuated to Fort Lauderdale and then returned for the cleanup of the hurricane's damage. Eventually, Al passed away and Connie carried on the business for a time. She said the hardest part was not having Al with whom to talk things over. Theirs had been a relationship built around his ideas, talking about them, planning and then working them out together.

Al and Connie had a long business partnership, with a strong marriage where both were supportive of the other.

If you're wondering about the Johnson's little girl, maybe you've guessed it—their daughter is Elaine, the co-author of this book.

The Best Is Yet To Come!

Your Business

Your Company Name

You and Your Spouse

(Be dedicated...work hard...enjoy it...enjoy and support each other...learn a lot...give great service...earn a proper profit!)

We said "The best is yet to come" because if it's right for the two of you to be in business together, you can look forward to great adventures ahead.

It may not be easy; in fact it might be pretty tough. However, if you have what it takes and want it enough, it can be terrific. The business could become a delight, and your marriage might be more fulfilling than you ever expected.

However, remember—as we said at the start of the book—being married…in business isn't for everyone. Only you can decide. Give it proper time and thought. Bring in the necessary experts to advise you. Then move forward in whichever direction is right for you.

THE S.C.O.R.E. OFFICES– COAST TO COAST!

Here we present a list of 389 S.C.O.R.E. offices (Service Corps of Retired Executives) from coast to coast. S.C.O.R.E. is a government-funded organization that brings people who need counseling regarding their small businesses together with qualified retired executives who are in a position to offer that counsel. It is a resource partner with the Small Business Administration (SBA). Locations and telephone numbers have been noted for your convenience. Feel free to get in touch with them.

Chapter Name	City	State	Phone
Anchorage SCORE	Anchorage	AK	(907) 271-4022
Mobile SCORE	Mobile	AL	(334) 433-6951
North Alabama SCORE	Birmingham	AL	(205) 934-6868
East Alabama SCORE	Opelika	AL	(334) 745-4861
Baldwin County SCORE	Fairhope	AL	(334) 928-8799
Tuscaloosa SCORE	Tuscaloosa	AL	(205) 758-7588
Northeast Alabama SCORE	Anniston	AL	(256) 237-3536
Shoals SCORE	Florence	AL	(256) 760-9067
Alabama Capitol SCORE	Montgomery	AL	(334) 240-6868
South Central SCORE	El Dorado	AR	(870) 863-6113
Garland County SCORE	Hot Springs	AR	(501) 321-1700
SE Arkansas SCORE	Pine Bluff	AR	(870) 535-7189
Ozark SCORE	Fayetteville	AR	(501) 442-7619
NW Arkansas SCORE	Fort Smith	AR	(501) 783-3556
Little Rock SCORE	Little Rock	AR	(501) 324-5893
East Valley SCORE	Mesa	AZ	(602) 379-3100
Lake Havasu SCORE	Lake Havasu City	AZ	(520) 453-5951
Phoenix SCORE	Phoenix	AZ	(602) 640-2329
Tucson SCORE	Tucson	AZ	(520) 670-5008
Yuma SCORE	Yuma	AZ	(520) 342-9443
Prescott Arizona SCORE	Prescott	AZ	(520) 778-7438
Antelope Valley SCORE	Quartz Hill	CA	(805) 272-0087
Sacramento SCORE	Sacramento	CA	(916) 361-2322
Tuolumne County SCORE	Sonora	CA	(209) 532-4212
Santa Clara Cty SCORE	San Jose	CA	(408) 288-8479
Central California SCORE	Fresno	CA	(209) 487-5605
San Luis Obispo SCORE	San Luis Obispo	CA	(805) 547-0779
Santa Rosa SCORE	Santa Rosa	CA	(707) 571-8342
Greater Chico Area SCORE	Chico	CA	(530) 342-8932
Palm Springs SCORE	Palm Springs	CA	(760) 320-6682

Chapter Name	City	State	Phone
Steinbeck-Roecker SCORE	Salinas	CA	(408) 422-5017
Central Coast SCORE	Santa Maria	CA	(805) 347-7755
Hemet SCORE	Hemet	CA	(909) 652-4390
Golden Empire SCORE	Bakersfield	CA	(805) 322-5881
East Bay SCORE	Oakland	CA	(510) 273-6611
Yosemite SCORE	Modesto	CA	(209) 521-9333
Stockton SCORE	Stockton	CA	(209) 946-6293
Los Angeles SCORE	Glendale	CA	(818) 552-3206
Shasta SCORE	Redding	CA	(530) 225-2770
Ventura SCORE	Ventura	CA	(805) 658-2688
Santa Barbara SCORE	Santa Barbara	CA	(805) 563-0084
San Diego SCORE	San Diego	CA	(619) 557-7272
Orange Cty SCORE	Santa Ana	CA	(714) 550-7369
San Francisco SCORE	San Francisco	CA	(415) 744-6827
Colorado Springs SCORE	Colorado Springs	CO	(719) 636-3074
Pueblo SCORE	Pueblo	CO	(719) 542-1704
Grand Junction SCORE	Grand Junction	CO	(970) 243-5242
Denver SCORE	Denver	CO	(303) 844-3985
Greater Danbury SCORE	Brookfield	CT	(203) 775-1151
Greater Bridgeport SCORE	Bridgeport	CT	(203) 576-4369
Fairfield Cty SCORE	Norwalk	CT	(203) 847-7348
Grtr Hartford Cty SCORE	Hartford	CT	(860) 548-1749
New Haven SCORE	New Haven	CT	(203) 865-7645
Old Saybrook SCORE	Old Saybrook	CT	(860) 388-9508
Washington DC SCORE	Washington	DC	(202) 606-4000
Wilmington SCORE	Wilmington	DE	(302) 573-6552
Ft. Lauderdale SCORE	Ft. Lauderdale	FL	(954) 356-7263
Treasure Coast SCORE	Ft. Pierce	FL	(561) 489-0548
Tallahassee SCORE	Tallahassee	FL	(850) 487-2665
Naples of Collier SCORE	Naples	FL	(941) 417-1280
Ocala SCORE	Ocala	FL	(352) 629-5959
Pasco County SCORE	New Port Richey	FL	(813) 842-4638
Lake-Sumter SCORE	Tavares	FL	(352) 365-3556
South Palm Beach SCORE	Delray Beach	FL	(561) 278-7752
Orlando SCORE	Orlando	FL	(407) 648-6476
Space Coast SCORE	Melbourne	FL	(407) 254-2288
Charlotte County SCORE	Punta Gorda	FL	(941) 575-1818
Jacksonville SCORE	Jacksonville	FL	(904) 443-1911
South Broward SCORE	Hollywood	FL	(954) 966-8415
Palm Beach SCORE	West Palm Beach	FL	(561) 833-1672
Hillsborough SCORE	Tampa	FL	(813) 870-0125
Central Florida SCORE	Lakeland	FL	(941) 619-5783
Manasota SCORE	Sarasota	FL	(941) 955-1029
Suncoast/Pinellas SCORE	Clearwater	FL	(813) 532-6800
Dade SCORE	Miami	FL	(305) 371-6889
Daytona Beach SCORE	Holly Hills	FL	(904) 255-6889
Gainesville SCORE	Gainesville	FL	(352) 375-8278
Citrus County SCORE	Homosassa	FL	(352) 382-1037
Southwest Florida SCORE	Fort Myers	FL	(941) 489-2935
Atlanta SCORE	Atlanta	GA	(404) 347-2442
Savannah SCORE	Savannah	GA	(912) 652-4335

Chapter Name	City	State	Phone
Dalton-Whitfield SCORE	Dalton	GA	(706) 279-3383
SCORE of Hawaii, Inc,	Honolulu	HI	(808) 522-8132
Iowa Lakes SCORE	Spencer	IA	(712) 262-3059
Des Moines SCORE	Des Moines	IA	(515) 284-4760
Sioux City SCORE	Sioux City	IA	(712) 277-2324
Council Bluffs SCORE	Council Bluffs	IA	(712) 325-1000
Cedar Rapids SCORE	Cedar Rapids	IA	(319) 362-6405
River City SCORE	Mason City	IA	(515) 423-5724
Waterloo SCORE	Waterloo	IA	(319) 233-8431
Burlington SCORE	Burlington	IA	(319) 752-2967
Fort Dodge SCORE	Fort Dodge	IA	(515) 955-2622
South Central SCORE	Ottumwa	IA	(515) 683-5127
Iowa City SCORE	Iowa City	IA	(319) 338-1662
Central Iowa SCORE	Marshalltown	IA	(515) 753-6645
Illowa SCORE	Clinton	IA	(319) 242-5702
Northeast Iowa SCORE	Cresco	IA	(319) 547-3377
Keokuk SCORE	Keokuk	IA	(319) 524-5055
Vista SCORE	Storm Lake	IA	(712) 732-3780
Dubuque SCORE	Peosta	IA	(319) 556-5110
Eastern Idaho SCORE	Idaho Falls	ID	(208) 523-1022
Treasure Valley SCORE	Boise	ID	(208) 334-1696
Greater Alton SCORE	Godfrey	IL	(618) 467-2280
Peoria SCORE	Peoria	IL	(309) 676-0755
Springfield SCORE	Springfield	IL	(217) 492-4416
Quad Cities SCORE	Moline	IL	(309) 797-0082
Northern Illinois SCORE	Rockford	IL	(815) 962-0122
Southern Illinois SCORE	Carbondale	IL	(618) 453-6654
Decatur SCORE	Decatur	IL	(217) 424-6297
Fox Valley SCORE	Aurora	IL	(630) 897-9214
Chicago SCORE	Chicago	IL	(312) 353-7724
Central Illinois SCORE	Bloomington	IL	(309) 664-0549
Quincy Tri-State SCORE	Quincy	IL	(217) 222-8093
Marion/Grant Co SCORE	Marion	IN	(765) 664-5107
Kokomo/Howard Co SCORE	Kokomo	IN	(765) 457-5301
Bloomington SCORE	Bloomington	IN	(812) 335-7344
S. Central Indiana SCORE	New Albany	IN	(812) 945-0266
Anderson SCORE	Anderson	IN	(765) 642-0264
Logansport SCORE	Logansport	IN	(219) 753-6388
Gary SCORE	Gary	IN	(219) 882-3918
South Bend SCORE	South Bend	IN	(219) 282-4350
Indianapolis SCORE	Indianapolis	IN	(317) 226-7264
Elkhart SCORE	Elkhart	IN	(219) 293-1531
Evansville SCORE	Evansville	IN	(812) 426-6144
Fort Wayne SCORE	Fort Wayne	IN	(219) 422-2601
South East Indiana SCORE	Columbus	IN	(812) 379-4457
Southwest Kansas SCORE	Dodge City	KS	(316) 227-3119
Wichita SCORE	Wichita	KS	(316) 269-6273
Salina SCORE	Salina	KS	(785) 243-4290
Emporia SCORE	Emporia	KS	(316) 342-1600
Ark Valley SCORE	Winfield	KS	(316) 221-1617
Topeka SCORE	Topeka	KS	(785) 231-1010

Chapter Name	City	State	Phone
Hutchison SCORE	Hutchison	KS	(316) 665-8468
McPherson SCORE	McPherson	KS	(316) 241-3303
Louisville SCORE	Louisville	KY	(502) 582-5976
Lexington SCORE	Lexington	KY	(606) 231-9902
Paducah SCORE	Paducah	KY	(502) 442-5685
New Orleans SCORE	New Orleans	LA	(504) 589-2356
Lake Charles SCORE	Lake Charles	LA	(318) 433-3632
Shreveport SCORE	Shreveport	LA	(318) 677-2536
Lafayette SCORE	Lafayette	LA	(318) 233-2705
Central Louisiana SCORE	Alexandria	LA	(318) 442-6671
North Shore SCORE	Hammond	LA	(504) 345-4457
NE Louisiana SCORE	Monroe	LA	(318) 323-0878
Baton Rouge SCORE	Baton Rouge	LA	(504) 381-7130
Worcester SCORE	Worcester	MA	(508) 753-2929
Bristol/Plymouth Co SCORE	New Bedford	MA	(508) 994-5093
NE Massachusetts SCORE	Danvers	MA	(978) 777-2200
Cape Cod SCORE	Hyannis	MA	(508) 775-4884
Boston SCORE	Boston	MA	(617) 565-5591
Springfield SCORE	Springfield	MA	(413) 785-0314
SE Massachusetts SCORE	Brockton	MA	(508) 587-2673
Salisbury SCORE	Salisbury	MD	(410) 749-0185
Frederick County SCORE	Frederick	MD	(301) 662-8723
Upper Shore SCORE	Easton	MD	(410) 822-4606
Southern Maryland SCORE	Annapolis	MD	(410) 266-9553
Baltimore SCORE	Baltimore	MD	(410) 962-2233
Hagerstown SCORE	Hagerstown	MD	(301) 739-2015
Lewiston-Auburn SCORE	Lewiston	ME	(207) 782-3708
Maine Coastal SCORE	Ellsworth	ME	(207) 667-5800
Oxford Hills SCORE	South Paris	ME	(207) 743-0499
Western Mountains SCORE	Rumford	ME	(207) 364-8122
Bangor SCORE	Bangor	ME	(207) 941-9707
Cen & N Arrostock SCORE	Caribou	ME	(207) 492-8010
Augusta SCORE	Augusta	ME	(207) 622-8509
Portland SCORE	Portland	ME	(207) 772-1147
Upper Peninsula SCORE	Sault Ste. Marie	MI	(906) 632-3301
Kalamazoo SCORE	Kalamazoo	MI	(616) 381-5382
Petoskey SCORE	Petoskey	MI	(616) 347-4150
Detroit SCORE	Detroit	MI	(313) 226-7947
Grand Rapids SCORE	Grand Rapids	MI	(616) 771-0305
Traverse City SCORE	Traverse City	MI	(616) 947-5075
SW Minnesota SCORE	Mankato	MN	(507) 345-4519
Minneapolis SCORE	Minneapolis	MN	(612) 591-0539
SE Minnesota SCORE	Rochester	MN	(507) 288-1122
St. Paul SCORE	St. Paul	MN	(612) 223-5010
South Metro SCORE	Burnsville	MN	(612) 898-5645
Duluth SCORE	Duluth	MN	(218) 723-2701
Central Area SCORE	St. Cloud	MN	(320) 240-1332
Lake Ozark SCORE	Camdenton	MO	(573) 346-2644
Poplar Bluff Area SCORE	Poplar Bluff	MO	(573) 686-8892
Kansas City SCORE	Kansas City	MO	(816) 374-6675
St. Louis SCORE	St. Louis	MO	(314) 539-6970

Chapter Name	City	State	Phone
Springfield SCORE	Springfield	MO	(417) 864-7670
Tri-Lakes SCORE	Kimberling City	MO	(417) 739-3041
Mid Missouri SCORE	Columbia	MO	(573) 874-1132
Mo-Kan SCORE	Webb City	MO	(417) 673-3984
St. Joseph SCORE	St. Joseph	MO	(816) 232-4461
Ozark-Gateway SCORE	Cuba	MO	(573) 885-4954
Lewis & Clark SCORE	St. Peters	MO	(314) 928-2900
Delta SCORE	Greenville	MS	(601) 378-3141
Gulfcoast SCORE	Gulfport	MS	(601) 863-4449
Butte SCORE	Butte	MT	(406) 494-3702
Kalispell SCORE	Kalispell	MT	(406) 756-5271
Helena SCORE	Helena	MT	(406) 441-1081
Missoula SCORE	Missoula	MT	(406) 327-8806
Great Falls SCORE	Great Falls	MT	(406) 761-4434
Billings SCORE	Billings	MT	(406) 245-4111
Havre SCORE	Havre	MT	(406) 265-4383
Bozeman SCORE	Bozeman	MT	(406) 586-5421
Greensboro SCORE	Greensboro	NC	(910) 333-5399
Charlotte SCORE	Charlotte	NC	(704) 344-6576
Hendersonville SCORE	Hendersonville	NC	(828) 693-8702
Asheboro SCORE	Asheboro	NC	(336) 626-2626
Wilmington SCORE	Wilmington	NC	(910) 815-4576
High Point SCORE	High Point	NC	(336) 882-8625
Durham SCORE	Durham	NC	(919) 541-2171
Sandhills Area SCORE	Southern Pines	NC	(910) 692-3926
Chapel Hill SCORE	Chapel Hill	NC	(919) 967-7075
Outer Banks SCORE	Kill Devil Hills	NC	(252) 441-8144
Down East SCORE	New Bern	NC	(252) 633-6688
Asheville SCORE	Asheville	NC	(828) 271-4786
Raleigh SCORE	Raleigh	NC	(919) 856-4739
Minot SCORE	Minot	ND	(701) 852-6883
Upper Red River SCORE	Grand Forks	ND	(701) 777-3051
Fargo SCORE	Fargo	ND	(701) 239-5677
Bismarck-Mandan SCORE	Bismarck	ND	(701) 250-4303
Lincoln SCORE	Lincoln	NE	(402) 437-2409
Omaha SCORE	Omaha	NE	(402) 221-3606
Columbus SCORE	Columbus	NE	(402) 564-2769
North Platte SCORE	Cozad	NE	(308) 784-2590
Hastings SCORE	Hastings	NE	(402) 463-3447
Panhandle SCORE	Minatare	NE	(308) 632-2133
Fremont SCORE	Fremont	NE	(402) 721-2641
Concord SCORE	Concord	NH	(603) 225-1400
Mt. Washington Va SCORE	Conway	NH	(603) 383-0800
Monadnock SCORE	Keene	NH	(603) 352-0320
Merrimack Valley SCORE	Manchester	NH	(603) 666-7561
Lakes Region SCORE	Laconia	NH	(603) 524-9168
Seacoast SCORE	Portsmouth	NH	(603) 433-0575
Upper Valley SCORE	Lebanon	NH	(603) 448-3491
Ocean County SCORE	Toms River	NJ	(732) 505-6033
Somerset SCORE	Somerville	NJ	(908) 218-8874
S New Jersey SCORE	Pennsauken	NJ	(609) 486-3421

Chapter Name	City	State	Phone
Bergen Cty SCORE	Paramus	NJ	(201) 599-6090
Monmouth SCORE	Lincroft	NJ	(732) 224-2573
North West SCORE	Hamburg	NJ	(973) 209-8525
Newark SCORE	Newark	NJ	(973) 645-3982
Greater Princeton SCORE	Princeton	NJ	(609) 520-1776
Las Cruces SCORE	Las Cruces	NM	(505) 523-5627
Albuquerque SCORE	Albuquerque	NM	(505) 766-1900
Roswell SCORE	Roswell	NM	(505) 625-2112
Santa Fe SCORE	Santa Fe	NM	(505) 988-6302
Las Vegas SCORE	Las Vegas	NV	(702) 388-6104
Northern Nevada SCORE	Reno	NV	(702) 784-4436
Utica SCORE	Utica	NY	(315) 792-7553
Suffolk SCORE	West Hampton Bch	NY	(516) 288-6340
Tompkins County SCORE	Ithaca	NY	(607) 273-7080
Clinton, Franklin, Essex	Plattsburgh	NY	(518) 563-1000
Nassau County SCORE	Mineola	NY	(516) 571-3303
New York SCORE	New York	NY	(212) 264-4507
Queens County SCORE	Kew Gardens	NY	(718) 263-8961
Ulster SCORE	Stone Ridge	NY	(914) 687-5035
Staten Island SCORE	Staten Island	NY	(718) 727-1221
Orange County SCORE	Goshen	NY	(914) 294-8080
Watertown SCORE	Watertown	NY	(315) 788-1200
Northeast SCORE	Albany	NY	(518) 446-1118
Dutchess SCORE	Poughkeepsie	NY	(914) 454-1700
Huntington Area SCORE	Huntington	NY	(516) 423-6100
S Tier Binghamton SCORE	Binghamton	NY	(607) 772-8860
Buffalo SCORE	Buffalo	NY	(716) 551-4301
Auburn SCORE	Auburn	NY	(315) 252-7291
Rochester SCORE	Rochester	NY	(716) 263-6473
Brookhaven SCORE	Medford	NY	(516) 451-6563
Westchester SCORE	White Plains	NY	(914) 948-3907
Chemung SCORE	Elmira	NY	(607) 734-3358
Syracuse SCORE	Syracuse	NY	(315) 471-9393
Toledo SCORE	Toledo	OH	(419) 259-7598
Licking County SCORE	Newark	OH	(614) 345-7458
Heart of Ohio SCORE	Wooster	OH	(330) 262-5735
Canton SCORE	Canton	OH	(330) 453-6047
Mansfield SCORE	Mansfield	OH	(419) 522-3211
Youngstown SCORE	Youngstown	OH	(330) 746-2687
Akron SCORE	Akron	OH	(330) 379-3163
Cincinnati SCORE	Cincinnati	OH	(513) 684-2812
Cleveland SCORE	Cleveland	OH	(216) 522-4194
Columbus SCORE	Columbus	OH	(614) 469-2357
Dayton SCORE	Dayton	OH	(937) 225-2887
Oklahoma City SCORE	Oklahoma City	OK	(405) 231-5163
Ardmore SCORE	Ardmore	OK	(405) 223-7765
Lawton SCORE	Lawton	OK	(580) 353-8727
Tulsa SCORE	Tulsa	OK	(918) 581-7462
NE Oklahoma SCORE	Grove	OK	(918) 786-6284
Southern Oregon SCORE	Medford	OR	(541) 776-4220
Willamette SCORE	Eugene	OR	(541) 465-6600

Chapter Name	City	State	Phone
Salem SCORE	Salem	OR	(503) 370-2896
Bend SCORE	Bend	OR	(541) 382-3221
Portland SCORE	Portland	OR	(503) 326-3441
Central PA SCORE	State College	PA	(814) 234-9415
Monroe -Stroudsbrg SCORE	Stroudsburg	PA	(717) 421-4433
Chester County SCORE	West Chester	PA	(610) 344-6910
Westmoreland Co SCORE	Latrobe	PA	(412) 539-7505
Cumberland Valley SCORE	Chambersburg	PA	(717) 264-2935
Bucks County SCORE	Fairless Hills	PA	(215) 943-8850
N. Central PA SCORE	Williamsport	PA	(717) 322-3720
Altoona-Blair SCORE	Altoona	PA	(814) 943-8151
Tri-County SCORE	Pottstown	PA	(610) 327-2673
Warren County SCORE	Warren	PA	(814) 723-9017
Mon-Valley SCORE	Monessen	PA	(412) 684-4277
Uniontown SCORE	Uniontown	PA	(724) 437-4222
York SCORE	York	PA	(717) 845-8830
Scranton SCORE	Scranton	PA	(717) 347-4611
Erie SCORE	Erie	PA	(814) 871-5650
Lehigh Valley SCORE	Bethlehem	PA	(610) 758-4496
Philadelphia SCORE	Philadelphia	PA	(215) 790-5050
Harrisburg SCORE	Camp Hill	PA	(717) 761-4304
Reading SCORE	Reading	PA	(610) 376-3497
E. Montgomery Cty SCORE	Jenkintown	PA	(215) 885-3027
Pittsburgh SCORE	Pittsburgh	PA	(412) 395-6560
Lancaster SCORE	Lancaster	PA	(717) 397-3092
Wilkes-Barre SCORE	Wilkes-Barre	PA	(717) 826-6502
PR & VI SCORE	San Juan	PR	(787) 766-5001
JGE Knight SCORE	Providence	RI	(401) 528-4571
Grand Strand SCORE	Myrtle Beach	SC	(803) 918-1079
Coastal SCORE	Charleston	SC	(803) 727-4778
Midlands SCORE	Columbia	SC	(803) 765-5131
Piedmont SCORE	Greenville	SC	(864) 271-3638
Sioux Falls SCORE	Sioux Falls	SD	(605) 330-4231
Rapid City SCORE	Rapid City	SD	(605) 394-5311
Jackson SCORE	Jackson	TN	(901) 423-2200
Memphis SCORE	Memphis	TN	(901) 544-3588
Nashville SCORE	Nashville	TN	(615) 736-7621
Chattanooga SCORE	Chattanooga	TN	(423) 752-5190
Greater Knoxville SCORE	Knoxville	TN	(423) 545-4203
NE Tennessee SCORE	Johnson City	TN	(423) 929-7686
Kingsport SCORE	Kingsport	TN	(423) 392-8805
Austin SCORE	Austin	TX	(512) 442-7235
Golden Triangle SCORE	Beaumont	TX	(409) 838-6581
Wichita Falls SCORE	Wichita Falls	TX	(940) 723-2741
Brazos Valley SCORE	Bryan	TX	(409) 776-8876
Waco SCORE	Waco	TX	(254) 754-8898
East Texas SCORE	Tyler	TX	(903) 510-2975
Lubbock SCORE	Lubbock	TX	(806) 472-7462
El Paso SCORE	El Paso	TX	(915) 534-0541
Corpus Christi SCORE	Corpus Christi	TX	(512) 888-4322
L Rio Grande Vly SCORE	Harlingen	TX	(956) 427-8533

Chapter Name	City	State	Phone
San Antonio SCORE	San Antonio	TX	(210) 472-5931
Fort Worth SCORE	Ft. Worth	TX	(817) 871-6002
Houston SCORE	Houston	TX	(713) 773-6565
Dallas SCORE	Dallas	TX	(214) 828-2471
Texarkana SCORE	Texarkana	TX	(903) 792-7191
Central Utah SCORE	Provo	UT	(801) 226-0881
Northern Utah SCORE	Logan	UT	(435) 752-2161
Southern Utah SCORE	St. George	UT	(801) 652-7741
Ogden SCORE	Ogden	UT	(801) 625-5712
Salt Lake SCORE	Salt Lake City	UT	(801) 364-1331
Tri-Cities SCORE	Hopewell	VA	(804) 458-5536
Peninsula SCORE	Hampton	VA	(757) 766-2000
Bristol SCORE	Bristol	VA	(423) 989-4850
Shenandoah Vly SCORE	Waynesboro	VA	(540) 949-8203
Central Virginia SCORE	Charlottesville	VA	(804) 295-6712
Greater Lynchburg SCORE	Lynchburg	VA	(804) 846-3235
Gr Pr. William Co SCORE	Prince William	VA	(703) 590-5000
Martinsville SCORE	Martinsville	VA	(540) 632-6401
Williamsburg SCORE	Williamsburg	VA	(757) 229-6511
Hampton Roads SCORE	Norfolk	VA	(757) 441-3733
Roanoke SCORE	Roanoke	VA	(540) 857-2834
Richmond SCORE	Richmond	VA	(804) 771-2400
Marble Valley SCORE	Rutland	VT	(802) 773-9147
Northeast Kingdom SCORE	St. Johnsbury	VT	(802) 748-5101
Montpelier SCORE	Montpelier	VT	(802) 828-4422
Champlain Valley SCORE	Essex Junction	VT	(802) 951-6762
Mid-Columbia SCORE	Yakima	WA	(509) 574-4944
Bellingham SCORE	Bellingham	WA	(360) 676-3307
Seattle SCORE	Seattle	WA	(206) 553-7320
Spokane SCORE	Spokane	WA	(509) 353-2820
Tacoma SCORE	Tacoma	WA	(253) 274-1288
Ft. Vancouver SCORE	Vancouver	WA	(360) 699-1079
Superior SCORE	Superior	WI	(715) 394-7388
Madison SCORE	Middleton	WI	(608) 831-5464
Eau Claire SCORE	Eau Claire	WI	(715) 834-1573
Fox Cities SCORE	Appleton	WI	(920) 734-7101
La Crosse SCORE	La Crosse	WI	(608) 784-4880
Wausau SCORE	Wausau	WI	(715) 845-6231
Green Bay SCORE	Green Bay	WI	(920) 496-8930
Central Wisconsin SCORE	Stevens Point	WI	(715) 344-7729
Milwaukee SCORE	Milwaukee	WI	(414) 297-3942
U Monongahela Va SCORE	Fairmont	WV	(304) 363-0486
Huntington SCORE	Huntington	WV	(304) 523-4092
Charleston SCORE	Charleston	WV	(304) 347-5463
Wheeling SCORE	Wheeling	WV	(304) 233-2575
Casper SCORE	Casper	WY	(307) 261-6529

Index

J

K

L

M

N

O

P

R

S

How to Contact the Authors

Jack and Elaine Wyman, the authors of this book, would like to know your thoughts about *Married...in Business.* Subject to their availability, the Wymans also participate in appropriate speaking engagements and seminars.

You may contact them by e-mail at wymco@aol.com.